W0172335

CAMDEN TOWN

Oberstufe

Qualifikationsphase

Erarbeitet von

Anne-Kathrin Böker

Florian Brauel

Alexander Kuhrs Woltin

Jana Oldendörp

Tom Schrock

Contents

Contents

1 📖 **SB p. 18**

Complete the crossword.

ACROSS

(4) Some countries are more … than others when it comes to legalizing abortion. (adj)

(6) Some issues, like the death penalty, are highly … (adj)

(7) opposite of "superior" (adj)

(8) … marriages are illegal in some countries. (adj)

(9) You can feel the … in the room when two opposing groups discuss central topics. (n)

(10) A common belief is that girls are often more … than boys. (adj)

(12) A person that has no contact to other people lives in … (n)

(13) Some religious communities have been … for their beliefs. (v)

(14) Some immigrants … quickly to fit in society. (v)

(15) If something is planned, it is … (adj)

(16) Some of my friends are of Arabic … (n)

(17) The most common … in Ireland is Catholicism. (n)

(18) a word that has a similar meaning as "to hide" (v)

DOWN

(1) Some animals cannot live together in … (e.g. cats and mice). (n)

(2) People might have divergent … of the same event. (n)

(3) The Republicans are usually more … than the Democrats. (adj)

(5) Aborigines are the … people of Australia. (adj)

(11) the history, traditions, buildings, and objects that a country or society has had for many years and that are considered an important part of its character (n)

2 📖 **SB p. 18**

CHALLENGE Read the WordPool text on p. 18 in your textbook again. Create a poster in which you graphically present the relation(s) between the individual and society. Prepare a short talk about your poster using as many words as possible from the crossword above.

Analysing narrative perspective

1   📖 **SB p. 24/4**

a) Read the statements. Which narrative perspective do they refer to? Tick (✔) the correct box.

statement	first-person narration	third-person narration	
		omniscient	selective
The narrator is usually a character in the story and speaks about him- or herself or shares events that he or she is experiencing.	❏	❏	❏
There is an all-knowing narrator who not only reports facts but may also reveal events, thoughts and feelings of any character, thus offering perspectives of multiple characters.	❏	❏	❏
The narrator reports facts and interprets events, thoughts, and feelings from the perspective of one single character.	❏	❏	❏
Using pronouns (e.g., "I", "me", "mine", "we", "us", "ours") invites the reader to become involved and identify with the narrator through subjective (biased) insights into his or her thoughts and feelings.	❏	❏	❏
The narrator knows how the plot will progress and can switch between places and times while narrating.	❏	❏	❏
While other characters are also referred to in the third person, only a single character is followed in depth (usually the main character).	❏	❏	❏
The story is told exclusively from inside the mind and feelings of one (main) character.	❏	❏	❏
The narrator is not a character in the story and has an unrestricted perspective.	❏	❏	❏
The narrator is not a character in the story and has a restricted perspective.	❏	❏	❏

b) Read the descriptions. Which mode of presentation do they describe? Tick (✔) the correct box.

Description: This mode of presentation ...	telling (panoramic mode)	showing (scenic mode)	stream of con- scious- ness
... illustrates the action by bringing the events into spatial and temporal proximity to the reader through detailed descriptions, just like a witness report. Dialogues and the reproduction of the characters' perceptions, thoughts and feelings are typical components, which convey intense moments vividly. This also creates an effect of immediacy.	❏	❏	❏
... attempts to describe events in the natural flow of thoughts in the mind of a character. It is an exploration of a character's mind in which the reader is directly introduced to his or her interior life. Thought processes or the actual experience of thinking in all its chaos and distraction can be portrayed, for example, by sudden mental leaps, incorporating sensory impressions, incomplete ideas, or unusual syntax.	❏	❏	❏
... summarizes selected events and gives a condensed overview of an event that takes place over a longer period of time. The reader is provided with an extensive and comprehensive view. Compression of time and ellipsis are common devices to create the impression of spatial and temporal distance from the action, which generates a feeling of distance to the events and characters for the reader.	❏	❏	❏

2 📖 **SB p. 26/4**

Read the following extracts from two Irish short stories. Examine for each of them the narrative perspective and the mode of presentation.

Extract 1

The Sugawn Chair
by Sean O'Faolain

Every autumn I am reminded of an abandoned sugawn chair[1] that languished[2] for years, without a seat, in the attic of my old home. It is associated in my mind with an enormous sack which the carter[3] used to dump with
5 a thud[4] on the kitchen floor around every October. I was a small kid then, and it was as high as myself. This sack had 'come up from the country', a sort of diplomatic messenger from the fields to the city. It smelled of dust and hay and apples, for the top half of it always bulged[5]
10 with potatoes, and, under a layer of hay, the bottom half bulged with apples. Its arrival always gave my mother great joy and a little sorrow, because it came from the farm where she had been born. Immediately she saw it she glowed with pride in having a 'back',
15 as she called it – meaning something behind her more solid and permanent than city streets, though she was also saddened by the memories that choked her with this smell of hay and potatoes from the home farm, and apples from the little orchard[6] near the farmhouse. My
20 father, who had also been born on a farm, also took great pleasure in these country fruits, and as the two of them stood over the sack, in the kitchen, in the middle of the humming city, everything that their youth had meant to them used to make them smile and laugh and use words
25 that they had never used during the rest of the year, and which I thought magical: words like late sowing[7], clover crop[8], inch field[9], marl[10] bottom, headlands[11], tubers[12], and the names of potatoes, British Queens or Arran Banners, that sounded to me like the names of regiments. For
30 those moments my father and mother became a young, courting[13] couple again. As they stood over the sack, as you might say warming their hands to it, they were intensely happy, close to each other, in love again. To me they were very old people. Counting back now, I reckon
35 that they were about forty-two or forty-three. [...]

Annotations
1 **sugawn chair** (n) – a chair with a seat made of straw rope
2 to **languish** (v) – to be forced to stay somewhere
3 **carter** (n) – someone whose job was to drive a cart in the past
4 **thud** (n) – the low sound made by a heavy object hitting something else
5 to **bulge** (v) – to stick out in a rounded shape, especially because something is very full or too tight
6 **orchard** (n) – a place where fruit trees are grown
7 to **sow** (v) – to plant or scatter seeds on a piece of ground
8 **clover crop** (n) – a great crop
9 **inch field** (n) – a reference to a small field to be found by a river or stream
10 **marl** (n) – soil consisting of lime and clay
11 **headland** (n) – an area of land that sticks out from the coast into the sea
12 **tuber** (n) – a round swollen part on the stem of some plants, such as the potato, that grows below the ground and from which new plants grow
13 to **court sb** (v) – to have a romantic relationship with somebody that you hope to marry

Language support

- The excerpt is a typical example of ... because ...
- The narrative perspective / The mode of presentation can be classified as ...
- This excerpt shows all the features of ...
- The story is told from the point of view of ...
- The narrator guides the reader by ... / comments on the events ... / presents X's thoughts and feelings ...
- The narrator views ... from a distance / stands back from the action and observes / remains outside the plot, merely observing.
- The story is narrated in the first / third person.
- The descriptions are restricted / limited.
- The narrator is a central character in the story.

Extract 2

This short story is set in Dublin during the early days of the Irish Civil War (1922-1923), which accompanied the establishment of the independent Irish Free State.

The Sniper
by Liam O'Flaherty

[...] On a rooftop near O'Connell Bridge, a Republican sniper[1] lay watching. Beside him lay his rifle and over his shoulders was slung a pair of field glasses. His face was the face of a student, thin and ascetic, but his eyes
5 had the cold gleam of the fanatic. They were deep and thoughtful, the eyes of a man who is used to looking at death.

He was eating a sandwich hungrily. He had eaten nothing since morning. He had been too excited to
10 eat. He finished the sandwich, and, taking a flask of whiskey from his pocket, he took a short drought. Then he returned the flask to his pocket. He paused for a moment, considering whether he should risk a smoke. It was dangerous. The flash might be seen in the darkness,
15 and there were enemies watching. He decided to take the risk. Placing a cigarette between his lips, he struck a match, inhaled the smoke hurriedly and put out the light. Almost immediately, a bullet flattened itself against the parapet[2] of the roof. The sniper took another whiff and
20 put out the cigarette. [...]

Cautiously he raised himself and peered over the parapet. There was a flash and a bullet whizzed over his head. He dropped immediately. He had seen the flash. It came from the opposite side of the street. [...] His enemy was
25 under cover.

Just then an armored car came across the bridge and advanced slowly up the street. It stopped on the opposite side of the street, fifty yards ahead. The sniper could hear the dull panting of the motor. His heart beat faster.
30 It was an enemy car. He wanted to fire, but he knew it was useless. His bullets would never pierce the steel that covered the gray monster.

Then round the corner of a side street came an old woman, her head covered by a tattered[3] shawl. She began to talk
35 to the man in the turret[4] of the car. She was pointing to the roof where the sniper lay. An informer.

The turret opened. A man's head and shoulders appeared, looking toward the sniper. The sniper raised his rifle and fired. The head fell heavily on the turret wall. The
40 woman darted toward the side street. The sniper fired again. The woman whirled round and fell with a shriek into the gutter[5]. [...]

Annotations
[1] **sniper** (n) – a person who shoots at somebody from a hidden position
[2] **parapet** (n) – a low wall along the edge of a bridge or a roof to stop people from falling
[3] **tattered** (adj) – old and torn; in bad condition
[4] **turret** (n) – Geschützturm
[5] **gutter** (n) – a channel at the edge of a road where water collects and is carried away to drains

_____

_____

_____

_____

_____

_____

_____

_____

_____

_____

1

Conditionals

3 📖 SB p. 26/5

To discuss different conditions in the past, present and future as well as their consequences, you use conditional sentences.

(A) Conditional 0: You use this structure to talk about things that are always true.
(B) Conditional I: You use this structure to talk about likely future possibilities.
(C) Conditional II: You use this structure to talk about improbable or imaginary situations in the present or future.
(D) Conditional III: You use this structure to talk about imaginary situations in the past with an unchangeable past result.

conditional structure	if-clause	main clause
0	simple present	simple present
I	simple present	will future
II	simple past	would + infinitive
III	past perfect	would + have + past participle

a) Match the sentences with the correct uses (A–D).

1. If Zee's religious community had been more tolerant, Zee and Conor would have had a relationship. ☐

2. If Conor appears at the bonfire, Zee will be irritated. ☐

3. Tasha would be glad if Zee spent time with Conor. ☐

4. If Zee talks to Conor, things start to turn for the worse. ☐

b) Correct the grammar mistakes in the following conditional sentences.
1. If Alissa had more time, she'll go and study in Australia.

_____

2. If you'll repeat a word several times, you will probably remember it.

_____

3. If Lisa had attended more lessons, she would passed the exams.

_____

4. If Zee, as a student, reads books in English, her vocabulary improved.

_____

c) To prepare your discussion (SB p. 26/5), note down five sentences in the conditional.

_____

_____

_____

_____

_____

Clichés and stereotypes

1   📖 **SB p. 28/1**

a) Read the info box. Then, decide whether the following sentences are **stereotypes (auto- or hetero-),
    prejudices** (often negative heterostereotypes) or **clichés**. Draw lines.

Stereotypes, prejudices and clichés

- A **stereotype** is an adjudgement[1] (in the sense of an opinion) that can be adopted about specific types
  of individuals or certain ways of doing things. These thoughts or beliefs may or may not reflect reality
  accurately. You can differentiate between:
  - an **autostereotype**, which is an adjudgement (in the sense of an opinion) that an ethnic group forms
    about itself. The autostereotype is often more differentiated than the heterostereotype. Positive
    attributes are dominating.
  - a **heterostereotype**, which is more an association, a prejudice used by an ethnic group to define others.
    Heterostereotypes tend towards the black-or-white pattern: stronger generalization or simplification.
- A **prejudice** is an unfair and unreasonable opinion or feeling, especially when formed without enough
  thought or knowledge.
- A **cliché** is a popular or common saying or remark that has lost originality and ingenuity by long overuse.

[1] **adjudgement** – pre-set opinion

autostereotype		Some foreigners believe: "All Germans are Nazis or fascists."
heterostereotype		An Italian man claims: "Italians are good lovers."
prejudice		A German friend of mine states: "All Latinos dance well."
cliché		The bride says: "My wedding day was just the happiest day of my life."

b) **Pair work** Compare your answer with a partner. Give reasons.

Listening

2   📖 **SB p. 28/3**   Webcode **DSW-73067-01**

a) Watch and listen to a video from the 1990s "What are the Germans like?" on different stereotypes the British have about the Germans (adjectives, features etc.). Take notes.

What are the Germans like?

b) Pair work Discuss with a partner about in how far you, as a person that lives in Germany in the 2020s, can or cannot identify with the clichés.

Mediation

3 📖 SB p. 30/4

A friend of yours, an American exchange student, wonders why there are no national flags in front of the school building. In contrast to the US, he believes that Germans tend to avoid showing their flag in public. After some research, you found the following newspaper article, which discusses whether German schools should raise the national flag. Write an e-mail to your friend in which you explain the different positions to him. Focus especially on the reasons for and against raising the national flag.

Die Welt, 27.11.2019

Soll vor unseren Schulen die deutsche Flagge wehen?

Spitzenpolitiker der Union fordern, vor Bildungsein-
richtungen Schwarz-Rot-Gold zu hissen. Ein wichtiges
Symbol, finden Anhänger der Idee. Reine Symbolpolitik,
meinen die Gegner. Unsere Autoren debattieren.

Ja, sagt Clemens Wergin
Wenn man in den USA lebt, ist es schwer, der amerikanischen Flagge zu entkommen. Sie weht vor Schulen, steckt in Vorgärten, und wenn wir von Washington
Richtung Annapolis ans Wasser fuhren, grüßte uns am
10 Autobahnrand eine mehrere Stockwerke große US-Fah-
ne, die majestätisch-getragen im Wind wogte. Die rot-
weiß gestreifte Flagge symbolisiert wie wenig anderes
den Drang der Amerikaner nach Freiheit und den Kampf
gegen die britischen Kolonialherren. [...]
15 Deutschland hat ein gebrochenes Verhältnis zu seinen
nationalen Symbolen. Entsprechende Skepsis hat die
Forderung der CDU ausgelöst, in Zukunft die deutsche
Flagge vor allen Schulen aufzuziehen. Tatsächlich war
das vor der deutschen Schule unserer Töchter in Wa-
20 shington längst gelebte Realität, wo die deutsche Flagge
einträglich neben der amerikanischen wehte. Was kei-
neswegs zu Ausbrüchen von gesteigertem Nationalismus
führte, wie nun viele befürchten.
Trotz der spürbaren Flaggen-Entkrampfung bei der
25 Fußball-WM 2006 steht das Herzeigen der Deutschland-
Fahne hierzulande weiter unter verschärftem Nationa-
lismusverdacht. Das sind Hemmungen, die durchaus
verständlich sind und die aus dem Zivilisationsbruch der
Nazi-Zeit erwuchsen.
30 Das Problem dabei: Die Fixierung auf die Nazi-Zeit ver-
stellt den Blick auf die positiven, liberalen Traditionen
der deutschen Geschichte. Und für diese steht Schwarz-
Rot-Gold wie wenige andere Symbole. Es waren die Far-
ben der deutschen Freiheitsbewegung, erst gegen die
35 Besatzung durch Napoleon, dann über Hambacher Fest
und Märzrevolution auch für die Etablierung einer Demokratie.
Ja, es stimmt, über lange Zeit hatte die Liberalität in
Deutschland keinen so sicheren Hafen gefunden wie in
40 den USA, [...]. Die schwarz-rot-goldenen Demokratieex-
perimente der Paulskirche und der Weimarer Republik
scheiterten. Aber der dritte Versuch mit amerikanischer
Hilfe war dann erfolgreich.

Nach sieben Jahrzehnten in Frieden und Freiheit ist die
45 Demokratie in der Bundesrepublik nicht mehr prekär
oder bedroht, sondern gelebte Selbstverständlichkeit.
Und für diese demokratische Tradition steht Schwarz-
Rot-Gold. Weshalb es an der Zeit ist, dass wir ein ent-
spannteres Verhältnis zu unserer Flagge bekommen. [...]
50 Und dazu gehören auch die Schulen, wo die nächste Generation von mündigen Bürgern erzogen wird, die hof-
fentlich die besten Traditionslinien der deutschen Geschichte in die Zukunft verlängern werden.

Nein, sagt Rainer Marx
55 Nationalflaggen sollen ein kulturelles Identifikations-
angebot an die Bürger eines Landes sein. Aber wodurch
wird diese Identifikation geschaffen? Durch die Flaggen?
Wohl kaum. Eine Fahne ist nur ein Symbol, ein Zeichen,
das ständig nach Bedeutung ringt. Für die einen ist
60 es das flatternde Alles, für die anderen ein hängendes
Nichts. Ein Stück Stoff an eine Holzlatte zu nageln und
„Deutschland, Deutschland" zu rufen, das kann – mit
Verlaub – jeder Depp.
Aber die gemeinsamen Wertvorstellungen aufzubauen,
65 die diesem Land zugrunde liegen, sie zu vermitteln, zu
pflegen, darum zu streiten, sie zu verteidigen und tag-
täglich auch zu leben, das ist die eigentliche Herausfor-
derung. Und dazu bedarf es keiner Symbole an Schulen,
sondern ganz klassischer Bildungs- und Erziehungsar-
70 beit. [...]
Darum sollte man den Vorschlag der CDU auch als das
bezeichnen, was er ist: reine Symbolpolitik. Statt sich
dafür starkzumachen, die Schulen personell und baulich
so auszustatten, dass sie ihrem Auftrag nachkommen
75 können, aus kleinen Menschen große Demokraten zu
machen, wählt man den bequemen Weg der Geste. Das
kostet nicht viel, hinterlässt aber viel Eindruck. Mit Fah-
nen vor Schulen aber schafft man keine neue Bildungs-
realität, man bedient nur den Patriotismus der Faulen.
80 Was wir unseren Kindern vermitteln sollten, ist genau
das Gegenteil: Dass nämlich die freiheitliche Verfassung
und die Form der Wertegemeinschaft, die wir hierzulande pflegen, nicht so leicht zu haben sind. Dass sie erwor-
ben werden müssen. Dass sie unabhängig von Nationa-
85 litäten sind. Dass jede Idee von Gemeinschaft größer ist
als das Zeichen, unter dem man sich versammelt. [...]

Rewriting a scene from a different perspective

1 📖 **SB p. 39/4**

a) Read the following extract from a Canadian short story. Briefly examine the narrative perspective and the mode of presentation and take some notes.

The Many Faces of Montgomery Clift
by Grace O'Connell

Lewin was named after his drunken grandfather and Micah was named for the Old Testament prophet who said, "Do not trust a neighbor; put no confidence in a friend," because Micah's mother had been both
5 converting and going through a bad time while pregnant. Her mother thought it was a girl's name when she saw it in the table of contents; she was new to the whole Bible thing, and it was an innocent mistake. But most people at John Huss Christian High School were named Joy
10 or Stacey or Matthew, and being a Micah meant there was a slight blurring around her, the smallest mark of strangeness that was sometimes enough to leave Micah feeling like there was a tiny satellite delay between herself and everyone around her, that she was isolated
15 one half-second ahead in time.

So she was intrigued to hear that a Lewin was transferring in. She had never heard the name before, and she pictured someone tall and thin, with a mean-looking mouth and tired eyes. When she saw Lewin for the first time, at his
20 father's funeral, he looked just like the picture in her head, so much so Micah thought she had, to a certain extent, invented him.

At the funeral, her mother told her to go and speak to him, to say she was sorry for his loss and that she
25 looked forward to having him in her class. She did this, and told Lewin about Bible Challenge, the Bible trivia competition that John Huss participated in along with the other Independent Christian schools in the region. "It's really fun," she said. "We get to go away for
30 tournaments. One of my teammates graduated, so maybe you can be on my team."

If this was an inappropriate conversation for a funeral, Micah didn't know, having never been to one. She hadn't known Lewin's father, but because Lewin was soon to be
35 a student at John Huss, Principal Garmash had activated the telephone prayer chain, and everyone had been told to go.

Lewin was examining a crustless cucumber-and-cream-cheese sandwich while Micah talked.

40 "I've already started studying," she said. "We're doing James first. It's short. But there's this one verse about the double-minded man that I know they'll have a ton of questions on."

Lewin didn't respond, but he moved his gaze from the
45 sandwich to Micah, so she went on.

"He looks in the mirror and forgets his own face. That's the verse."

Lewin said, "He has two faces?"

"No, he's double-minded, not double-faced." [...]

_____

_____

_____

_____

_____

_____

_____

b) **Creative writing** Rewrite the scene at the funeral from either Lewin or Micah's point of view using first-person narration.

Gender identity

1 📖 **SB p. 42/1**

Love is love and comes in many forms and facets. For a long time, there was talk of LGBTQ+. This acronym has now been extended as follows: LGBTQQIP2SAA and stands for lesbian, gay, bisexual, transgender, queer, questioning, intersex, pansexual, two-spirit (2S), androgynous, and asexual. Match each term with the correct description.

	term		description
1	lesbian	A	... describes the lack of a sexual attraction or desire for other people.
2	gay	B	... describes people who naturally (without any medical interventions) develop primary and / or secondary sex characteristics that do not fit neatly into society's definitions of male or female.
3	bisexual	C	... describes a woman who is emotionally, romantically, or sexually attracted to other women.
4	transgender	D	... describes a person who is not limited in sexual choice with regard to biological sex, gender, or gender identity.
5	queer	E	... describes a person who is emotionally, romantically, or sexually attracted to members of the same gender.
6	questioning	F	... describes a third gender found in some Native American cultures, often involving birth-assigned men or women taking on the identities and roles of the opposite sex. A sacred and historical identity, which can include but is by no means limited to LGBTQ identities.
7	intersex	G	... describes a person who is emotionally, romantically, or sexually attracted to more than one sex, gender, or gender identity though not necessarily simultaneously, in the same way or to the same degree.
8	pansexual	H	... describes people who are in the process of exploring their sexual orientation or gender identity.
9	two-spirit (2S)	I	... refers to people identifying and / or presenting as neither distinguishably masculine nor feminine.
10	androgynous	J	... is seen as an umbrella term for people whose gender identity and / or expression is different from cultural expectations based on the sex they were assigned at birth. However, it does not imply any specific sexual orientation. These people may identify as straight, gay, lesbian, bisexual, etc.
11	asexual	K	... is a term people often use to express fluid identities and orientations.

1	2	3	4	5	6	7	8	9	10	11

2 Pair work 📖 **SB p. 44/4**

The government of Canada states the following:
"Canada stands up for the protection and promotion of the human rights of lesbian, gay, bisexual, transgender, queer, 2-spirit and intersex (LGBTQ2I) people globally. The human rights of all persons are universal and indivisible [...] regardless of their sexual orientation and their gender identity and expression."

Discuss Canada's legal attitude towards the LGBTQ2I community with a partner. Have you heard of different laws and / or legal accounts from other countries?

1

Non-fictional transgender report

3 📖 SB p. 43/3

Jessie is in her late 30s and lives on the Canadian prairies. Jessie is a heterosexual male bigender woman. That means that Jessie was born male, is heterosexual as Jessie has a girlfriend, and has two genders: Jessie is a man and a woman, depending on the day. However, Jessie spends most of her life living as a woman.

a) Read Jessie's blogpost and describe her feelings and fears related to dressing up as a woman for Halloween.

b) Compare Jessie's feelings and thoughts about Halloween with Peter's in the fictional story "For today I am a boy".

c) In contrast to Peter/Dana, Jessie does not fear any physical harm as "gay bashing" is not common in her living area. Do some research on gay bashing and explain what it means. Discuss possible measures to prevent gay bashing with a partner.

◁ ◉ ▷   🔍   ▽ ⌂

En Femme Halloween

September 29, 2012
Posted in Commentary, Uncategorized

Halloween is fast approaching and as we all know is the greatest day of the year for crossdresser; it's like having a pride parade without having to come out of the closet or is it reveal the rest of our closet?
5 Now admittedly I have not been out en femme for Halloween in a few years which, as we know, is a cardinal sin in our community, however I have my reasons.
– I have been worried about some of my friends'
10 reactions. I don't have any homophobe friends, not all are the most comfortable either, and I'm not gay but for some reason people that are completely comfortable with homosexuality are very disturbed by crossdressing. I would prefer not to create too
15 many issues though this is ridiculous as some of the costumes in the circles I run are really offensive.
– Crossdressing isn't a joke to me and I don't want to make it one. I feel compelled to do a reasonable
20 job of crossdressing as it is an expression of me. However at 6'3" 260 lbs I'll always look a bit ridiculous but I choose not to make my dressing a joke either.
– What happens if I do too good of a job? Looking
25 good in a dress is one thing but the silicone breast forms, padded panties, size 16 heels, the authentic corset and the not cheap wig all show that perhaps I am better at this then I should be and as I have said I am out to certain people, not all.
30 – Then we have the Facebook issue where I'm tagged in photos for my whole family and several coworkers to see in women's clothing.
But I have decided this year that it's about time for me to find my balls, push them up to where from
35 once they came, puff my silicone enhanced chest out and hold my made up head high as I step out for All Hallows' Eve. […]
This decision has some risk associated with it but the worst possible thing that could happen is
40 I'm outed for all the world to see and I lose some friends, have to put up with some bullshit from the others, some strange looks at work and have uncomfortable family dinners at holidays. I am not concerned about anyone attempting to cause me
45 physical harm as first gay bashing is rare here and as stated I'm a large imposing man. Basically I'm looking at possible social and familial alienation and the frustration of filling out a police report with press on nails. I would be injured but would survive
50 to fight another day. Worst case scenario if I don't go en femme this year is I miss yet another year of socially acceptable crossdressing where I can have a fun time enjoying fully who I am. I know you're expecting me to say that not going out is worse,
55 however it isn't, truly total social annihilation sucks. […]

Languages and identity

4 📖 **SB p. 45/3**

a) Look at the map and do some research on Switzerland and its languages. How does multilingualism affect the Swiss sense of identity?

Languages of Switzerland
- GERMAN
- FRENCH
- ITALIEN
- ROMANH

Similar to Canada, Switzerland has several national languages (German, French, Italian and Romansh). In contrast to German, French and Italian, which maintain equal status as official languages at the national level, Romansh is only used in dealings with people who speak the language. Nevertheless, the canton of "Graubünden" in the east is officially trilingual as most of the Romansh-speaking native population lives there.

b) Creative writing

Now write an elevenie (a short poem with a given structure) which expresses Switzerland's extraordinary situation with regard to its official languages. Be prepared to present your poem in class.

Info

The typical structure of an elevenie is as follows:

row	number of words	content
1	1	A noun: a thought, a topic, an object, a colour, a feeling, …
2	2	What does the word from the first row do?
3	3	Where or how is the word from the first row?
4	4	What do you think about it?
5	1	Conclusion: What results from all this? What is the outcome?

Title: _____

c) Compare the situation in Switzerland regarding languages and identity to the one in Canada.

WordPool — Science and technology

1 📖 **SB p. 48**

Complete the sentences using the words on the right.

> artificial | (to) coin | contentious | countless | device | (to) envision | extensive

1. The novel *Nineteen Eighty-Four* _____ the phrase "Orwellian state", a state with

   constant surveillance.

2. In the past 20 years _____ dystopian novels and films were published.

3. Another word for "controversial" is _____.

4. Despite _____ measures in the COVID-19 pandemic, hundreds of thousands of

   people died from the virus.

5. Another word for "imagine" is _____.

6. Many electronic _____ today make our houses smart homes.

7. The opposite of "natural" is _____.

2 📖 **SB p. 48**

On pp. 48-49 in your textbook there are a lot of useful words for writing and talking about science and technology, respectively about visions of the future. Look at the table and fill in the missing word classes. Use the provided language support on the right or consult a dictionary. Some words cannot be put into all categories.

Language support

Typical adjective suffixes: -able/-ible; -al; -ful; -ic; -ive; -less; -ous
Typical adverb suffixes: mostly, adverbs can be formed by adding -ly to an adjective
Typical noun suffixes: -al; -ation/-tion; -sion; -ment; -age; -ing

noun	verb	adjective/adverb
	(to) count	
enhancement		
		extensive/ly
	(to) resemble	
		(un)predictable/predictably
progress		
		constituted
		manipulable
supervision		
	(to) reproduce	
development		
		advanced
comprehension		

Tenses

3 📖 **SB p. 48**

Fill in the gaps using the correct tense. If you can find signal words, mark them first.

People have always liked to speculate about the future. In 1516, Sir Thomas More _____

(envision) a very optimistic future in his work *Utopia*. Long before that, the Greek and the Romans

_____ (speculate) about the future. But not only philosophers _____

(think) about what our future might bring. Also, authors of popular fiction _____ (invent)

many stories in the last 150 years. A well-known example is Frenchman Jules Verne, whose stories

_____ (inspire) many generations. One of his stories _____ (depict)

the life of the outcast Captain Nemo, who roams the oceans in a submarine called *Nautilus*. The novel

_____ (publish) in 1871. In the 1980s, Robert Zemeckis' film trilogy *Back to the Future*

_____ (be) a big box office hit. Since then, it _____ (entertain) many

generations. It is a more humorous approach to the topic. Even if many of its predictions for the year 2015

looked over-the-top in 1985, some of them _____ (become) reality.

In recent years, dystopian novels with female heroines in particular _____ (become) popular.

There is hardly any doubt that *visions of the future* _____ (be) popular in the future, too.

4 📖 **SB p. 48**

Fill in the gaps in the conversation with the correct future form.

Peter: Have you ever thought about what our lives _____ (be) like in 20 years?

Paula: I'm sure technology _____ (advance). I hope I _____ (drive) an

electric and autonomous car.

Peter: I _____ (live) in Sweden or in Norway. Scandinavian countries have always

been progressive and when you look at all the windmills they have already built, I'm sure they

_____ (support) the use of sustainable energy in the future.

Paula: I just hope that climate change _____ (not / affect) us as badly as scientists expect.

Peter: Yes, I think that _____ (be) a big issue. Well, but as technology and science advance,

perhaps they _____ (invent) things to tackle these problems.

Understanding and summarizing texts

1 📖 **SB p. 53/6**

The introductory sentence of a summary should answer the wh-questions: who, when, where, what type of text and what topic (see p. 330 in your textbook). Have a look at the beginning of the article below and complete the introduction of the summary.

The text _____ (*What is the title?*) is an ___*article*___

(*What type of text is it?*) by British journalist _____ (*Who is the author?*), published

in _____ (*Where was it published?*) on _____ (*When was it

published?*). It deals with _____ (*What does the text deal with?*).

2 📖 **SB p. 53/6**

a) Read the article and follow the instructions in the boxes. Take notes.

b) Sum up the paragraphs by taking notes next to the text. Underline or highlight words and phrases you consider important.

DORIAN LYNSKEY   The Guardian, 9 Oct 2019

'Alexa, are you invading my privacy?' – the dark side of our voice assistants

There are more than 100m Alexa-enabled devices in our homes. But are they fun time-savers or the beginning of an Orwellian nightmare?

> **Before you continue reading:** What do the heading and subheading reveal about the article? Anticipate what the article could be about and what the author's message might be.
>
> _____
>
> _____
>
> _____
>
> _____

[...] [V]oice assistants often do things that they are not supposed to do. Last year, an Amazon customer in Germany was mistakenly sent about 1,700 audio files from someone else's Echo[1], providing enough information to name and locate the unfortunate user and his girlfriend.
5 (Amazon attributed this "unfortunate mishap" to human error.)
In San Francisco, Shawn Kinnear claimed that his Echo activated itself and said cheerfully: "Every time I close my eyes, all I see is people dying." In Portland, Oregon, a woman discovered that her Echo had taken it upon itself to send recordings of private conversations to one of her
10 husband's employees. In a statement, Amazon said that the Echo must have misheard the wake word, misheard a request to send a message, misheard a name in its contacts list and then misheard a confirmation to send the message, all during a conversation about hardwood floors. Not great, Alexa.

Annotations
[1] **Amazon Echo –** smart speaker by US company Amazon which uses the voice assistant Alexa

Stop and think: After having read a paragraph actively, work with the text by asking yourself questions. Possible questions here:

What have I learned about voice assistants so far (reliability, data protection, the company's statements about failing devices)?

_____

_____

What does the author probably imply by starting his article with that information?

_____

_____

What may his message be?

_____

_____

How could the article go on?

_____

_____

Take notes, underline unknown words, mark statements you consider important with a text marker. Write questions, summaries or symbols next to the text. This helps you get a deeper understanding of the text and it will help you dealing with the summary and analysis later on.

15 Technology frequently inspires ambivalence: we know that Facebook and Google know too much about us, yet we continue to use their services because they're so damn convenient. Voice assistants, however, are unusually polarising. People who consider them sinister[2] and invasive[3] (myself included) regard enthusiasts as complacent[4], while those who
20 find them useful and benign see the sceptics as paranoid technophobes[5]. There is one question freighted with bigger issues about our relationship with the tech industry: should you let Alexa into your home?

Stop and think: What question does the author raise? _____

_____

In January, Amazon [...] revealed that the company had sold more than 100m Alexa-enabled devices. [...] Alexa, however, has grown up in an
25 era of increasing scepticism about the power and morality of the "big five" tech companies: Amazon, Apple, Facebook, Google/Alphabet and Microsoft. [...] Tech journalists are more likely to be critics than cheerleaders. Politicians are more willing to hold companies to account. This year has been particularly tricky. [Different media platforms have]
30 revealed that all the big five have been using human contractors[6] to

Annotations
[2] **sinister** (adj) – evil, bad
[3] **invasive** (adj) – tending to intrude on a person's privacy
[4] **complacent** (adj) – self-satisfied
[5] **technophobe** (n) – someone who is afraid of technology

Annotations
[6] **human contractor** (n) – here: employee listening to the input customers gave to the voice assistants

analyse a small percentage of voice-assistant recordings. Although the recordings are anonymised, they often contain enough information to identify or embarrass the user – particularly if what they overhear is confidential medical information or an inadvertent sex tape. The
35 revelations were the last straw for many Alexa sceptics. "We live in a techno-dystopia of our own making. If you still have an Alexa or any other voice assistant in your home, you were warned," wrote the Gizmodo[7] writer Matt Novak.

Annotations

[7] **Gizmodo** – a science and technology web portal

Stop and think: What attitude towards the big five do people have according to Lynskey?

_____

_____

What was the problem with the companies using human contractors?

_____

[Recently,] [r]ecordings began showing up as evidence in court cases. The
40 FBI refused to confirm or deny that it was using Alexa for surveillance purposes. "It became increasingly clear to me that the privacy watchdogs were right," [the Gizmodo editor] says. "It is, at base, a wiretapping device[8]."

[...] "You are building an infrastructure that can be later co-opted
45 in undesirable ways by large multinationals and state surveillance apparatus, and compromised by malicious hackers," says Dr Michael Veale, a lecturer in digital rights and regulation at UCL Faculty of Laws at University College London. [...] [Journalist and editor Marc] Rotenberg agrees: "If you're an authoritarian country, why not just run
50 the audio stream straight to a government surveillance agency and argue that it's to reduce crime in the home? It's scary to contemplate[9], but conceivable[10]." [...]

Annotations

[8] **wiretapping device** (n) – a device used to overhear alleged criminal activity

[9] to **contemplate** (v) – to consider

[10] **conceivable** (adj) – imaginable

Stop and think: What is data acquired through voice assistants supposedly used for?

_____

(Not in the text, but a question you could now ask yourself: What measures could the author now name that could be undertaken to stop these processes?)

_____

_____

The US government has been reluctant to act. [...] Without effective regulation, there is no defence against more invasive exploitation of
55 voice assistants. By definition always on, even when they are not awake, the devices are constantly listening, although not always transmitting. Dr Jeremy Gillula, [a campaigner against the misuse of technology,] says that there are no technical obstacles to enabling dormant devices to, for example, track users' television viewing by responding to high-
60 pitched signals embedded in shows and advertisements, or identify who is in the house at any given time. "That essentially becomes constant surveillance," Gillula says. "I am hopeful that the companies would never go down this dystopian path, but I could see them saying: 'Oh, it's a

feature: know when your kids are home!' An appealing feature is how
65 most of these things start."

> **Stop and think:** What does Gillula mean by "constant surveillance"?
>
> _____

Where they end up has galvanised[11] not just privacy watchdogs but writers. The dystopian implications of voice assistants are appearing in science fiction, including the Spike Jonze movie *Her, Black Mirror* and *Years and Years*. Behind them all looms the "never-sleeping ear" of
70 George Orwell's telescreen in *Nineteen Eighty-Four*: "You had to live – did live, from habit that became instinct – in the assumption that every sound you made was overheard." The Echo Show, a smart assistant with a screen and camera, was widely compared to the telescreen when it was introduced two years ago. [...]

Annotations
[11] to **galvanise sb** (v) – jdn wachrütteln

> **Stop and think:** What questions come up? _____
>
> _____
>
> How could the author end his article? _____
>
> _____

75 Today, voice assistants are not the most pressing threat to privacy only because they are optional. A facial recognition scanner can spy on you in a public space, but Alexa, like a vampire, must be invited into your home. The only truly effective power you can wield over this technology is not to use it. [...]
80 None of the people I spoke to owns a home voice assistant, nor would they advise anyone to get one, but they all agree that it would be possible to develop a device that delivers the most popular services while respecting the user's privacy. If the entire industry were to follow Apple's lead in making human monitoring opt-in rather than opt-out, that would be a
85 strong start. Then, as processing power increases, more tasks could be performed inside the device. But, of course, that would mean forfeiting that juicy, monetisable data. [...]

> **Stop and think:** How does the author answer his question from the beginning? What message does he have?
>
> _____
>
> _____
>
> _____
>
> _____

3   📖 **SB p. 53/6**

Now sum up the article in a coherent text. Use the introduction from task 1.

2

Mediation

1   📖 **SB p. 59/3**

Your American friend Bob is doing research for his school project on artificial intelligence (AI). He has heard that Germans are more sceptical than Americans when it comes to the use of AI. He has come across the article on the next page. In an e-mail give him a hand at understanding

a) how the attitude of the Germans towards AI has changed in the last few years,

b) in which areas they can imagine the use of AI,

c) in which areas they see problems and why.

Take some notes first, using the boxes below.

a)

b)

c)

René Schmöl   OWL am Sonntag, 18.10.2020

Weniger Vorbehalte gegen Künstliche Intelligenz (KI)

Umfrage: Große Skepsis bei selbstfahrenden Verkehrsmitteln

Computer, die schlauer als Menschen sind und Arbeitsplätze vernichten, gehören zu den realen Ängsten der Menschen in Deutschland. Gleichwohl stehen sie den Anwendungen von Künstlicher Intelligenz
5 (KI) nicht mehr so skeptisch gegenüber wie noch vor drei Jahren.

Einer Studie zufolge werden „Roboter-Autos" jedoch kritisch gesehen. Bei der jüngst in Berlin veröffentlichten Umfrage des Digitalverbandes Bitkom sagten
10 etwa zwei Drittel (68 Prozent), dass sie KI eher als Chance sehen. 29 Prozent der Befragten sagten, dass sie KI eher als Gefahr einschätzen. Bei einer Umfrage im Jahr 2017 lagen Befürworter und Skeptiker noch gleichauf.
15 Die Akzeptanz von KI variiert aber stark nach Einsatzgebiet. So befürworten 75 Prozent der Menschen in Deutschland einen Einsatz in der Pflege, 73 Prozent in Ämtern und Behörden, 67 Prozent in der Medizin und 54 Prozent in den Personalabteilungen. Dabei
20 befürchtet allerdings knapp die Hälfte der Befragten (49 Prozent), dass eine KI Bewerber ohne sachlichen Grund ablehnt, weil etwa der Algorithmus bestimmte Personen diskriminiere. Bei der Betreuung von Kleinkindern sind nur 38 Prozent der Meinung, dass
25 KI eingesetzt werden sollte. Umstritten ist die Frage, welche Rolle KI im Verkehr spielen soll. Drei Viertel (76 Prozent) gehen davon aus, dass sich KI-unterstützte Warnsysteme im Auto in den kommenden zehn Jahren durchgesetzt haben werden. 60 Prozent rech-
30 nen innerhalb von zehn Jahren mit dem Durchbruch selbstfahrender Busse auf den Straßen. Aber nur 44 Prozent erwarten selbstfahrende U- oder S-Bahnen,

39 Prozent Fernzüge und 37 Prozent selbstfahrende Lieferwagen. Autonome Autos können sich 30 Pro-
35 zent innerhalb von zehn Jahren auf deutschen Straßen vorstellen. Autonom fliegende Passagierflugzeuge in den nächsten zehn Jahren erwarten dagegen nur sechs Prozent, obwohl in diesem Bereich Autopilot-Systeme bereits eine Rolle spielen.
40 Wenn die KI im Auto komplett das Steuer übernimmt, sehen viele Menschen schwarz: Nur jeder Dritte (36 Prozent) sagt, selbstfahrende Autos würden schwere Unfälle und viele Tote vermeiden. Aber deutlich mehr (57 Prozent) gehen davon aus, dass es durch selbstfah-
45 rende Autos vermehrt zu schweren Unfällen mit vielen Toten kommen wird. „Dabei ist gerade die zusätzliche Sicherheit einer der wichtigsten Gründe für die Entwicklung autonomer Fahrzeuge", sagte Bitkom-Präsident Achim Berg. Er verwies auf die amtliche
50 Unfallstatistik: „Aktuell werden 9 von 10 Unfällen mit Verletzten oder Toten in Deutschland durch menschliches Fehlverhalten verursacht."

Berg forderte einen Kurswechsel beim Umgang mit Daten, damit Deutschland eine weltweite Führungs-
55 rolle bei Künstlicher Intelligenz einnehmen könne. „Datenverfügbarkeit und Datensouveränität müssen als Leitbild die Datensparsamkeit ersetzen", sagte der Bitkom-Präsident. Forderungen nach einer eigenständigen KI-Regulierung zeugten von einem falschen
60 Bild von Künstlicher Intelligenz. „Regulierung sollte immer eine Anwendung und ihre Auswirkungen betreffen, nicht die Technologie als solche", betonte Berg. „Wir brauchen keinen Algorithmen-TÜV."

Speaking about biohacking and cyborgs

2 📖 **SB p. 60/2**

Cyborgs and biohacking have been topics of a great variety of novels and films.

a) **Pair work** Describe the film stills on the next page and speculate to what extent the depicted people are cyborgs. Take turns.

b) **Pair work** Read the synopses. Explain which film or series you would like to watch.

c) Discuss which of the ideas and concepts about cyborgs are most likely to be developed in the future. Explain which ones you personally find worth striving for or morally doubtful.

d) Imagine you were a filmmaker or author. What cyborg story would you bring onto the screen or write about?

> Useful words:
> exoskeleton | implant |
> enhanced | (to) modify |
> (to) replace | biohacking |
> cortical stack | plug |
> hybrid | chip |
> prosthesis/prosthetics |
> application | augmentation |
> autonomous | sensory |
> nano technology | body
> modification | bionic

The Six Million Dollar Man (TV series 1973–1978)

The TV series *The Six Million Dollar Man* from the 1970s is based on the novel *Cyborg* by Martin Caidin. After a crash, astronaut Steve Austin's life is on the line. In a million-dollar operation his life is saved and organs are replaced with bionic implants which allow him to run faster, see objects in far distances and become inhumanly strong.

Star Trek – The Next Generation (Paramount Pictures 1987–1994)

In Gene Roddenberry's *Star Trek – The Next Generation* the ship's lieutenant Geordi La Forge is blind. He wears a visor that allows him to see and later in the series the visor is replaced with implants.

RoboCop (Metro-Goldwyn-Mayer 1987)

The science-fiction action film *RoboCop* is set in Detroit in the near future. The city has a massive crime problem and the company OCP develops robots to help fight the crimes. After police officer Alex Murphy has died in the line of duty, OCP turns him into a crime-fighting man-machine called RoboCop with an exoskeleton.

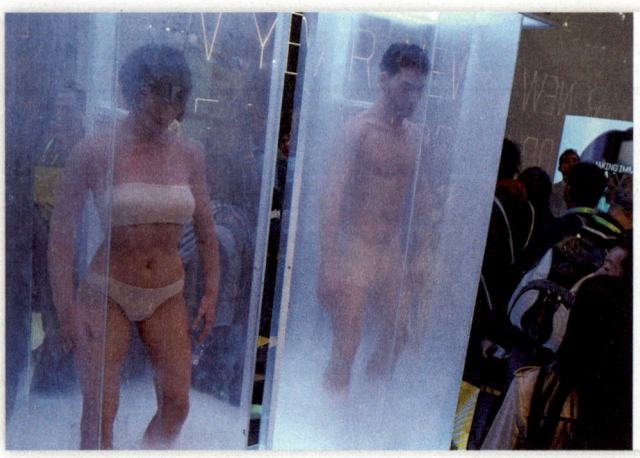

Altered Carbon (Netflix Streaming Services 2018)

In the novel *Altered Carbon* by Richard Morgan (2002), which in 2018 was turned into a TV series, bodies have become mere "sleeves". Memory and consciousness are downloaded onto a cortical stack in the spine. People who can afford the expensive technology grow clones and basically live forever replacing the "used sleeve" with a new one.

Analysing atmosphere

PRE-READING

1 📖 SB p. 62/1

You have probably heard of the terms and expressions "Big Brother", "Big Brother is watching you" or "Orwellian state". Describe (or take a guess) what a world with a Big Brother could look like.

_____

_____

_____

COMPREHENSION

2 📖 SB p. 62/2

Read the extract from George Orwell's novel *Nineteen Eighty-Four* and describe the world Winston Smith lives in.

Extract:

Nineteen Eighty-Four
by George Orwell, London 1949

Part 1, Chapter 1

[...] The hallway smelt of boiled cabbage and old rag mats. At one end of it a coloured poster, too large for indoor display, had been tacked to the wall. It depicted simply an enormous face, more than a metre wide: the
5 face of a man of about forty-five, with a heavy black moustache and ruggedly[1] handsome features. Winston made for the stairs. It was no use trying the lift. Even at the best of times it was seldom working, and at present the electric current was cut off during daylight hours.
10 [...] The flat was seven flights[2] up, and Winston, who was thirty-nine and had a varicose ulcer[3] above his right ankle, went slowly, resting several times on the way. On each landing, opposite the lift-shaft, the poster with the enormous face gazed from the wall. It was one of those
15 pictures which are so contrived that the eyes follow you about when you move. BIG BROTHER IS WATCHING YOU, the caption beneath it ran.
Inside the flat a fruity voice was reading out a list of figures which had something to do with the production
20 of pig-iron[4]. The voice came from an oblong[5] metal plaque like a dulled mirror which formed part of the surface of the right-hand wall. [...] The instrument (the telescreen, it was called) could be dimmed, but there was no way of shutting it off completely. He moved over to
25 the window: a smallish, frail figure, the meagreness[6] of his body merely emphasized by the blue overalls which were the uniform of the party. His hair was very fair, his face naturally sanguine, his skin roughened by coarse soap and blunt razor blades and the cold of the winter
30 that had just ended.

Outside, even through the shut window-pane, the world looked cold. Down in the street little eddies[7] of wind were whirling dust and torn paper into spirals, and though the sun was shining and the sky a harsh blue, there
35 seemed to be no colour in anything, except the posters that were plastered everywhere. [...] There was one on the house-front immediately opposite. BIG BROTHER IS WATCHING YOU, the caption said, while the dark eyes looked deep into Winston's own. [...] In the far distance a
40 helicopter skimmed down between the roofs, hovered for an instant like a bluebottle[8], and darted away again with a curving flight. It was the police patrol, snooping into people's windows. The patrols did not matter, however. Only the Thought Police mattered.
45 [...] The telescreen received and transmitted simultaneously. Any sound that Winston made, above the level of a very low whisper, would be picked up by it, moreover, so long as he remained within the field of vision which the metal plaque commanded, he could
50 be seen as well as heard. There was of course no way of knowing whether you were being watched at any given moment. [...]. [They] [...] could plug in your wire whenever they wanted to. You had to live – did live, from habit that became instinct – in the assumption that every
55 sound you made was overheard, and, except in darkness, every movement scrutinized. [...]

Annotations
[1] **rugged** (adj) – raw, rough
[2] **flight** (n) – floor
[3] **varicose ulcer** (n) – Krampfadern
[4] **pig-iron** (n) – raw iron
[5] **oblong** (adj) – rectangular
[6] **meagreness** (n) – skinniness
[7] **eddies** (n) – whirls
[8] **bluebottle** (n) – a certain kind of fly

Info

Nineteen Eighty-Four

Nineteen Eighty-Four is the archetype of a dystopian novel. Published in 1949 and set in a not-so-distant future, it depicts the story of protagonist Winston Smith, who lives in an England that is part of a totalitarian superstate called Oceania. "Big Brother" is the face of this regime, and a total surveillance is supposed to make sure that nobody opposes the system. When Smith starts to doubt the system, he must fear the totalitarian party's revenge.

Since the publication of *Nineteen Eighty-Four*, the term "Orwellian State" stands for an inhumane totalitarian state with constant surveillance.

ANALYSIS

3   📖 **SB p. 65/5**

a) In the following diagram, fill in information from the text about the setting / circumstances and about the characters and how this contributes to the atmosphere. Give lines references.

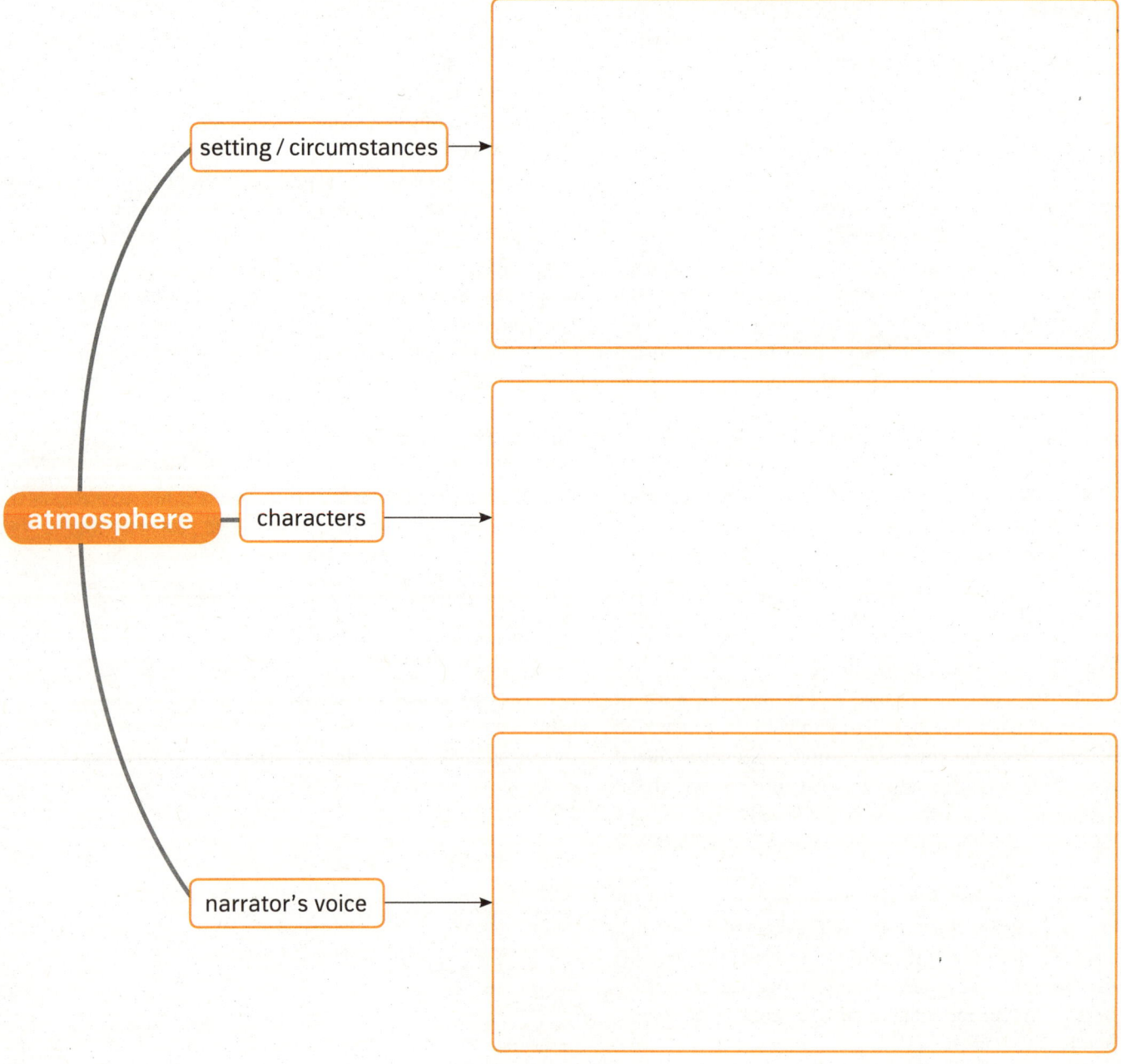

b) Examine the choice of words and stylistic means used by Orwell and their effect on the reader. Note down your observations in the last box of the diagram on p. 28.

c) Using your results from the diagram, analyse the atmosphere in the extract.

- The author makes use of / uses ... to create a / an ... atmosphere.
- The author employs stylistic devices to ...
- The use of long / short sentences / adjectives and adverbs with a positive / negative connotation / ... underlines / supports / enhances / affirms the message that ...
- A collection of adjectives to describe an atmosphere:
  Negative: uncanny | gloomy | violent | barren | pessimistic | alarming | suspenseful | scary | lonely | tense | ...
  Positive: cheerful | ecstatic | optimistic | peaceful | warm | light-hearted | hopeful | ...

WRITING: CREATIVE WRITING

4 EXTRA

Write a diary entry in which Winston Smith reflects on his miserable everyday life (see textbook p. 332 for help).

WRITING: COMMENT

5 EXTRA

Starting with Orwell's concept and examples of dystopia from the lessons, comment on whether our society already shows traits of a dystopian society or not. Refer to the concept of a dystopia as well as to work done in class.

_____

_____

_____

_____

_____

_____

_____

_____

_____

_____

_____

Life in the future

1 📖 **SB p. 68/1**

Think about how you envision the future. Write down negative visions into the dark parts and positive ideas and imaginations into the light parts of the yin and yang. Mark that sometimes a positive vision also has a downside. For example: in the future people may have enough to eat and there might be a sufficient health service for everyone (light), but this can lead to overpopulation (dark).

2 **Pair work** 📖 **SB p. 68/1**

Dystopian fiction almost always deals with an element of 'extrapolation'. This is an element of today's society that we already encounter but which the author extrapolates to warn us of future developments.

a) Introduce the 'dark side' of your visions of the future in task 1 to a partner.

b) Discuss which of your dark scenarios are more probable than others.

c) Discuss what problems and challenges of today's society already resemble those depicted in dystopian novels.

Analysing characters

PRE-READING

3 📖 **SB p. 68/2**

Imagine there was the possibility to totally suppress feelings (e.g. anger or fear). What advantages and disadvantages would that have?

COMPREHENSION

4 📖 **SB p. 68/2**

Read the extract from the novel *Do Androids Dream of Electric Sheep?*. Describe Rick and Iran's lives and the dystopian world they live in.

Extract:

Do Androids Dream of Electric Sheep?
by Philip K. Dick, 1968

Do Androids Dream of Electric Sheep? is a novel set on a near-future planet Earth which has suffered the events of a catastrophic third world war. With the technological advance, most of humanity has moved to colonies on other planets. In this extract Iran and her husband Rick talk about their "mood organ", which allows them to "dial" a mood they want to be in.

[...] "My schedule for today lists a six-hour self-accusatory[1] depression," Iran said.

"What? Why did you schedule that?" It defeated the whole purpose of the mood organ. "I didn't even know
5 you could set it for that," he said gloomily.

"I was sitting here one afternoon," Iran said, "and naturally I had turned on 'Buster Friendly and His Friendly Friends'[2] [...] and then that awful commercial came on, the one I hate. [...] And so for a minute I shut
10 off the sound. And I heard the building, this building; I heard the –" She gestured.

"Empty apartments," Rick said. Sometimes he heard them at night when he was supposed to be asleep [in the only] one-half occupied conapt[3] building [...].

15 "[W]hen I had the TV sound off, I was in a 382 mood; I had just dialed it. So although I heard the emptiness intellectually, I didn't feel it. My first reaction consisted of being grateful that we could afford a Penfield[4] mood organ. But then I realized how unhealthy it was, sensing
20 the absence of life, not just in this building but everywhere, and not reacting – do you see? I guess you don't. [...] So I left the TV sound off and I sat down at my mood organ and I experimented. And I finally found a setting for despair." Her dark, pert[5] face showed satisfaction, as if
25 she had achieved something of worth. "So I put it on my schedule for twice a month; I think that's a reasonable amount of time to feel hopeless about everything, about staying here on Earth after everybody who's smart has emigrated, don't you think?" [...]

Annotations
[1] **self-accusatory** (adj) – selbstanklagend
[2] **Buster Friendly and his Friendly Friends** – name of a TV show
[3] **conapt** (n) – word coined by Philip K. Dick from 'condominium' and 'apartment'
[4] **Penfield** – company that produces the mood organ
[5] **pert** (adj) – frech, schnippisch, kess

ANALYSIS

5 📖 SB p. 68/2

Characterize Iran. Pay attention to the language she uses, but also to the narrative perspective used by the author Philip K. Dick (see textbook pp. 352-353 for help).

> Tip When you are asked to characterize a protagonist, it is always useful to consider what the author had in mind when he came up with the narrative perspective he tells the story in.

_____

_____

_____

_____

_____

_____

_____

EVALUATION

6 📖 SB p. 69/3

Discuss in how far *Do Androids Dream of Electric Sheep?* is a typical dystopia and compare it to other dystopian worlds you know.

1 Modal verbs 📖 SB p. 76

a) Have a look at the grid and fill in the translation or the substitute forms (past and future).

modal verb	translation	substitute
must	müssen	to have to past: had to future: will have to
must not	nicht dürfen	not to be allowed to past: _____ future: _____
can		to be able to past: was / were able to future: will be able to
cannot / **can't**	nicht können, nicht fähig sein	not to be able to past: _____ future: _____
may		to be allowed to past: was / were allowed to future: will be allowed to
need not	nicht müssen	not to have to past: _____ future: _____

shall /
should /
ought to
		to be supposed to; to be expected to
		past: was / were supposed to;
		    was / were expected to
		future: will be supposed to;
		    will be expected to

b) Complete the sentences with a modal verb.

1. (Social) media _____ influence people's opinion.

2. Online news _____ be true because fake news is widespread.

3. You _____ use social media to connect and communicate with other individuals.

4. Social media platforms _____ save and share your personal data but they often do.

5. Responsible journalists _____ research well before publishing articles in printed

   newspapers while anybody _____ post his or her opinion as universal truth on online

   platforms.

6. Some people believe that media _____ be an all-pervasive part of everyday life.

7. You _____ use the possibilities of the internet to view the world from various political

standpoints.

c) Imagine it is the year 2000. People don't know much about social media and its impacts yet but
experts are already making some predictions. Write sentences 1–5 from task a) in the future tense.

1. _____

2. _____

3. _____

4. _____

5. _____

_____

2 📖 **SB p. 76**

Using the information and vocabulary provided on p. 76 in your textbook, think of five to ten rules or tips
when dealing with (social) media. Use modal verbs.

_____

_____

_____

_____

_____

_____

_____

3 📖 **SB p. 76**

Identify the following
phonetic transcriptions.

/ˈbrɔːdˌkɑːst/		/ˈædvə(r)taɪz/	
/ˈlɪt(ə)rəsi/		/ˈælgəˌrɪð(ə)m/	
/tekˈnɒlədʒi/		/fəˈnɒmɪnən/	

Media literacy

1 SB p. 78/2

a) Read the text on p. 79 in your textbook again. Visualize the influence different factors (e.g. mass media, friends) have on the individual's opinion. Think about how to present the factors' diverging degrees of pervasiveness. You can use the box on the right.

b) **Pair work** Showcase your visualization and explain it to a partner.

WRITING

2 SB p. 78/3

You think "media literacy" should at least be an elective subject in school. Use the information on pp. 78-79 in your textbook, including the media literacy concept, to convince the headmaster of your school.

You can either

• write a formal letter to your headmaster (see textbook p. 334 for help)

OR

• prepare a speech for the next school assembly (see textbook p. 337)

OR

• write a blog post for the school website (see textbook p. 340).

Language support

How to be convincing

Introduction: Catch attention!
• Recently there was a discussion about …
• The discussion about …
• Nowadays … / There are … / People …

Main part: State your point, explain it, use examples!
• My personal view is that … because …
• From my point of view …
• In my opinion …
• It may be argued that …
• The central / main argument …
• Another argument for / against is …
• Another point for / against is …
• The pro / contra argument is …
• On the one hand …, on the other hand …
• Moreover, I think …
• Next … / Finally … / Furthermore …
• Additionally one can say …

• It should be mentioned / seen / taken into consideration that …
• Also, it should be considered that …
• Another powerful / important argument is that …
• An example for this argument is …
• … is a good example for that (argument).

Conclusion: Sum up!
• In conclusion, you / one can say that …
• What it comes down to is that …
• That means …
• Looking at both sides I would say …
• Considering these facts, I think …
• As a result / consequence …
• With respect to the arguments above, I am of the opinion that …
• In summary, one can say …
• To sum it up, … / In summary …
• In a nutshell, …

LISTENING

3 SB p. 78/3   **Webcode** DSW-73067-02

Not only media literacy but also "digital literacy" is a crucial competence given our digital age. Listen to the University of Derby's introduction to "Digital literacy and why it matters" and answer the questions on p. 35. You do not need to write complete sentences.

1	How is 'digital literacy' defined?	
2	Most of the graduate jobs require 'ICT' skills. What are they and why are they important?	
3	What are the benefits of using digital media in educational settings? (State three benefits.)	
4	Which obligatory prerequisites go along with digital literacy? (State two responsibilities.)	
5	Why do digital literacy skills become increasingly more necessary? (Name two aspects.)	

Working with statistics

4 📖 **SB p. 80/1**

Your American e-pal is working on a project on how young people around the world inform themselves about current social and political issues. She asks you to answer this question for young people living in Germany. You have found a decent statistic on the internet, which you mediate to your friend in an email.

Language support

Reconsult pp. 80 and 362 in your textbook for help.

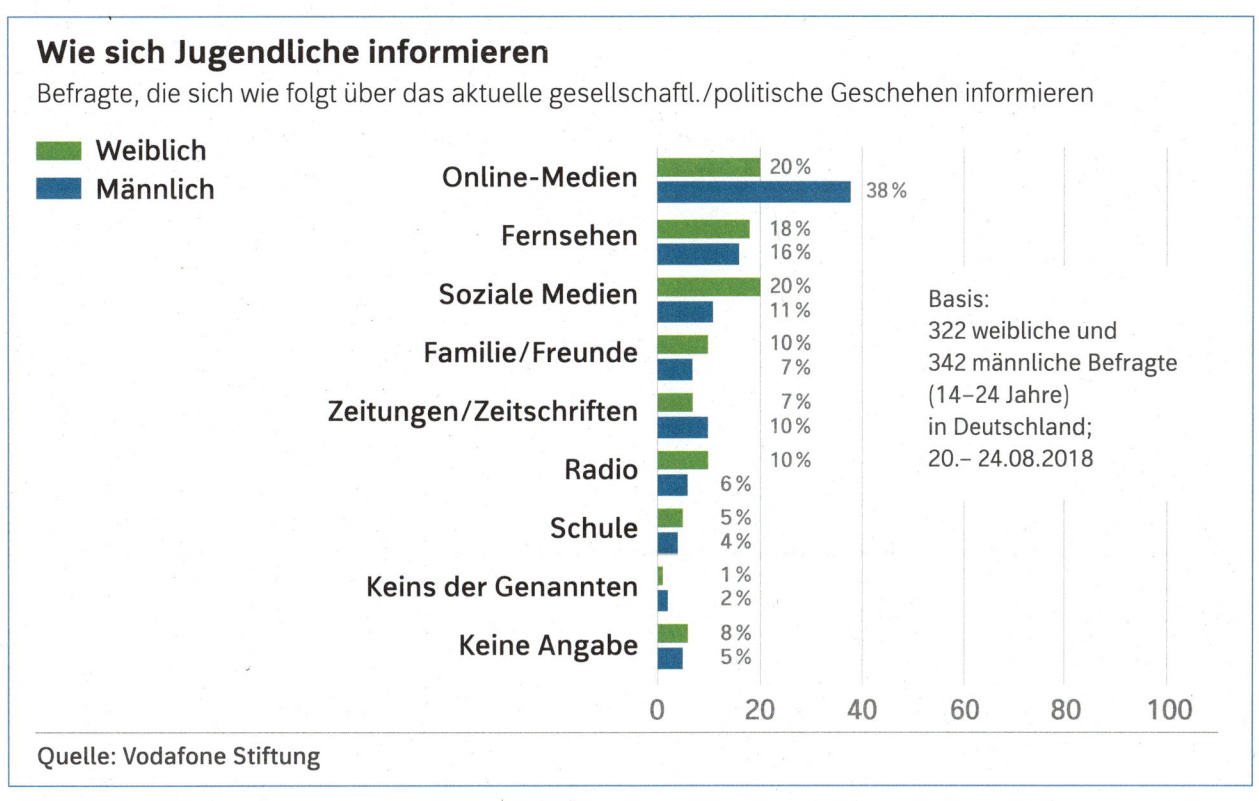

Wie sich Jugendliche informieren

Befragte, die sich wie folgt über das aktuelle gesellschaftl./politische Geschehen informieren

■ Weiblich
■ Männlich

Online-Medien 20 % / 38 %
Fernsehen 18 % / 16 %
Soziale Medien 20 % / 11 %
Familie/Freunde 10 % / 7 %
Zeitungen/Zeitschriften 7 % / 10 %
Radio 10 % / 6 %
Schule 5 % / 4 %
Keins der Genannten 1 % / 2 %
Keine Angabe 8 % / 5 %

Basis:
322 weibliche und
342 männliche Befragte
(14–24 Jahre)
in Deutschland;
20.– 24.08.2018

0   20   40   60   80   100

Quelle: Vodafone Stiftung

Fake news

1 📖 **SB p. 84/1**

a) Read the following headlines and decide whether they are real or fake. Note down a brief explanation.

		real	fake
a	Canadian zoo fined after taking bear out for ice-cream		
b	Fourteen elephants get drunk on corn wine and pass out in tea plantation		
c	Mysterious 7-foot creature spotted in Argentina		
d	Police in Germany rescue man chased by baby squirrel		
e	Teenager on trial after refusing to pay fine for feeding a chip to a pigeon		
f	83-year-old woman trains 65 cats to steal from her neighbours		

b) Pair work Discuss your results with a partner. Why do you think the headlines are real or fake? Do you have enough information to make an educated guess?

c) Check the solutions on p. 121 to see if you were right or wrong.

2 📖 **SB p. 84/1**

a) Read the two news flashes. Then read the additional information and decide whether each news flash is real or fake.

Title: **BREAKING NEWS:** **President's grandfather was a member of KKK[1]**	Title: **Teenager with 2-meter-long hair decides to get a bald cut**
A great deal of evidence leads to the assumption that the President's grandfather was an active participant in various racist-motivated attacks on people of color.	Mary holds the Guinness World Record for having the longest hair on a teenager. After years without cutting her hair, she decided to get a bald cut. Her reason: she wants to donate her hair to children suffering from cancer.
Published by: online media website called IP (impeachpresident)	**Published by:** New York Times
Other stories published by this website: • *High-speed ufo wants to attack the earth – President does nothing* • *President's wife has fake hair of fur* • *Climate change is a Chinese invention*	**Other stories published by this website:** • *Thomas Cook Travel company collapses* • *Hurricane destroys large parts of East coast cities* • *FridaysForFuture campaign continues*
Other websites that reported on this story: • The Daily Mirror, UK news company: *Evidence that attacks President's grandfather is insufficient* • Frankfurter Allgemeine Zeitung, German newspaper: *Gegner der Regierung verbreiten falsche Gerüchte* • WeAgainstThem, a propaganda website: *Truth revealed – President is child of a KKK member*	**Other websites that reported on this story:** • CNN, a TV news programme: *Helping children beats Guinness World Record – Teenager cuts her hair for good reason* • The Guardian, a UK news company: *Teenager helps children with cancer to get beautiful wigs* • Süddeutsche Zeitung, German newspaper: *Teenager lässt Haare 13 Jahre lang wachsen, um krebskranken Kindern neue Hoffnung zu geben*

[1] **KKK** – Ku Klux Klan is a racist and violent terrorist group that has been active in the Southern States of the US

b) **Pair work** Discuss your answer with a partner. Give reasons.

c) Note down questions you could ask yourself to differentiate fake news from real news. Then prepare a "fact-check flyer".

> **Tip** You can use modal verbs in your flyer.

_____

_____

_____

_____

_____

_____

_____

Film analysis: *The Social Network*

1 📖 **SB p. 86/1**

Film posters, DVD covers, and trailers provide a selected visual preview trying to catch and arouse the potential target groups' interest to advertise and promote a film. Using the film poster as a starting point, first describe it and then speculate about the content, genre and the potential audience of *The Social Network* (2010). Give reasons.

Info

Examples of film genres:

- action
- crime
- documentary
- drama
- fantasy
- horror
- romance
- suspense / mystery

Language support

Description / layout:
- The film poster shows / illustrates / depicts …
- In the poster / In the picture I can see …
- There is / are / seems to be …
- One can see …
- The field size is a close-up / medium shot / long shot …
- The layout emphasizes …
- The layout is rather detailed / simple with …
- The focus of attention …
- What strikes the eye is the key / main image / the image of … taking up the most space.
- There is a contrast between …
- A contrast is clearly recognizable / visible.

Language:
- Use the simple present BUT use the present progressive when referring to actions in the picture.
- Use specific descriptive expressions (e.g. on the left / at the bottom).
- Use suitable adjectives and adverbs.
- Employ linking words / connectives.

Content / genre:
- When looking at the film poster, I think / feel / am reminded of …
- Initially the image makes me think / gives the impression of …
- The choice of colours supports the idea of / suggests / contributes to …
- The film's mood and tone are reflected / illustrated by …
- It can be assumed that … because …
- … is a symbol of …
- The film poster appeals to audiences that enjoy films containing dramatic tension / showing male views of the world / depicting the topic of protecting law and order, right and wrong / focusing on one protagonist, powerful and ready to take on the enemy / …
- The film poster depicts / shows / portrays / represents / illustrates / conveys … which is why I believe / think that …

2 📖 **SB p. 86/3**

a) Look at the following film stills from *The Social Network* and describe them by focusing on different cinematic devices like field size, camera angle and point of view.

_____

_____

_____

_____

b) Considering your previous findings with regard to the film poster in task 1, revisit your ideas about the content/genre and check if you need to change anything about your ideas.

_____

_____

_____

3 📖 **SB p. 88/4**   Webcode DSW-73067-03

a) Watch the trailer of *The Social Network*. Check whether your assumptions and predictions in tasks 1–2 were right or wrong.

_____

_____

b) Analyse how the trailer presents the formation of Facebook as the birth of an idea that reorganized the mechanisms of society even though it unraveled the friendship of the creators, by focusing on the following aspects:
- the editing / montage (see language support below)
- the background music
- contrast of online vs. real life

> **Tip** If you want to read the lyrics of the song:
> Webcode **DSW-73067-04**

Language support

Editing / montage:
- cut (fast / slow cuts): fast cuts create a vividness of the action; slow cuts create focus on sth specific or create calmness
- fade in / fade out: opens / closes an action or scene slowly
- cross-cut: focusses on contrast and thus creates suspense
- slow motion: intensifies an action or a moment
- fast motion: intensifies speed creating the impression of change
- voice-over: a commenting, narrating and/or explaining voice (of a character) that is not on-screen
- flashback / flash forward: changes chronological order and therefore connects / disconnects action or moments
- floating, superimposed text: focusses on text and its meaning, gives additional information without adding voices or stressing the meaning of voices

Info

Music/sound:
- diegetic: sounds from 'the world inside' the film, e.g. conversation, window closing, footsteps
- non-diegetic: sounds from 'the world outside' the film, e.g. film music, sounds creating suspense
- voice-over (off-camera commentary): non-diegetic information by a narrator

Function:
- to build up suspense
- to show a certain mood / create a certain atmosphere
- to describe a character
- to foreshadow an event

Social media apps

PRE-READING

1   📖 SB p. 90/1

a) **Group work** Are you using Facebook? Why or why not?
   Discuss.

b) Now examine the cartoon and evaluate it (language
   support see p. 361 in your textbook).

"What are the kids up to? I can't
find them on here anywhere..."

COMPREHENSION

c) Read Sweney and De Liz's article and explain why teenage users are leaving Facebook.

MARK SWENEY AND ANA DE LIZ   The Guardian, 16 February 2018

'Parents killed it': why Facebook is losing its teenage users

This year more than 3 million under-25s in the UK and US are expected to leave the site

When Mark Zuckerberg launched Facebook he was a 19-year-old living in a dorm in his second year at university. Fast-forward 14 years and it is the young people he was so successful in luring[1] to
5 Facebook to propel it to become the world's biggest social networking site that are now his biggest problem.

This year more than 3 million under-25s in the UK and US will either quit Facebook or stop using it
10 regularly, and they are pretty vocal[2] about why.

"As soon as parents got in they killed it," says 24-year-old Jordan Ranford, a now minimal Facebook user who ditched his mum as a friend because she was "just jarring[3]".
15 Georgia Davey, 21, predicts a bleak[4] future for the increasingly uncool Facebook. "I don't know if I should say this, but I think Facebook might shut down one day," she says. "There will be a new thing soon and no one will be on it any more."
20 With 2 billion registered users it is impossible to see Facebook closing. But her comment highlights an inherent truth of internet life: impermanence[5]. Digital businesses age in dog years, meaning today's new thing can rapidly become yesterday's
25 news. Anyone remember MySpace or Second Life? Facebook is managing to keep a proportion of disaffected youngsters: many have moved to Instagram, which it bought in 2012 for $1bn, but the big winner is increasingly Snapchat. About
30 44% of Snapchat users are aged 18 to 24, while just 20% of Facebook's are now in that key age range,

according to Ampere Analysis.

The youth exodus is being balanced by older users joining, and the first users of Facebook are
35 moving into their 30s and 40s. As a result, there will be an increase of about 3.6m over-35s in the US and UK this year, according to eMarketer. But the mass departure of younger users has prompted questions about whether the world might now be
40 at peak Facebook.

"I don't know about calling peak Facebook globally but one of Facebook's biggest challenges is that it is saturating[6] core markets, western markets, where it has really slowed down," says Richard Broughton,
45 an analyst at Ampere. "Most of the population likely to go on it are on it."

Facebook has become a vast money-making machine. Its revenues rocketed 47% to nearly $41bn last year and its profits soared 56% to nearly $16bn.
50 But its advertising-based business model is also proving to be its Achilles heel.

Flooding users' timelines with more and more commercial messages may please investors – Facebook's advertising dominance has pushed the
55 company's stockmarket value past $522bn – but it is being unfriended by its user base.

Last month, Zuckerberg responded by cleaning up its news feed algorithm to prioritise what friends and family share, and reducing the amount of non-
60 advertising content from publishers and brands, which he said were "crowding out the personal moments". He said the company was focused on

Annotations
[1] to **lure** (v) –
to attract customers
[2] **vocal** (adj) –
outspoken
[3] **jarring** (adj) –
making someone
feel annoyed or
shocked
[4] **bleak** (adj) – without
anything to make
you feel happy or
hopeful
[5] **impermanence** (n) –
temporary state, not
staying the same
forever
[6] to **saturate** (v) –
to put a lot of
something into a
particular place,
especially so that
you could not add
any more (German:
sättigen)

"making sure the time we all spend on Facebook is time well spent".

65 "The fundamental confusion with Facebook is that it increasingly talks about itself as a community platform, but that is not the reality," says Benji Vaughan, chief executive at Disciple Media. "Do users feel part of a community when they are 70 there? I have reservations about whether they do. Facebook's core purpose is to sell targeted content to individuals. All its issues begin there."

Zuckerberg admitted recently that 2017 was a "hard one", with the company taking a beating on 75 all sides.

Politicians have attacked Facebook over its role in disseminating[7] fake news. Earlier this month UK MPs grilled the company's executives in an evidence session in its own backyard in the US. 80 Concerns continue to be raised over Facebook's use as a platform for Russian meddling[8] in the US elections.

This week Unilever, maker of brands from Marmite to Magnum and the world's second-biggest 85 advertiser, threatened to withdraw its advertising from Facebook and YouTube unless they cleaned up the "swamp" of opaque business practices and dodgy[9] content.

Zuckerberg has his work cut out attempting to 90 navigate Facebook through its awkward teenage years. Still just 33, with 60% voting power, he is far from ready to throw in the towel.

"They are in an innovator's dilemma, seen as the monolithic[10] rigid media company," says Fergus 95 Hay, chief executive of the ad agency Leagas Delaney.

"No one would bet against Zuckerberg, but Facebook needs to grow out of [relying on advertising] or the hipster will be dad on the dancefloor."

100 **Georgia Davey, 21**

"I'm still on Facebook to keep in touch with old friends, to plan meet-ups and just … to be nosey," says Georgia. But she thinks it is becoming a platform "for the old generation to sort of keep an 105 eye on the younger generation – that's why I don't really post many things there". For her, "Instagram is much more interesting because it's more visual and I relate more to photos than words".

Facebook, she says, now seems to be a platform for 110 advertisements, "but it's also an easier way to find news and articles from magazines, as opposed to having to look through their websites. […]"

**Viktoria Valchanova, 17, and
Alina Postelnicu, 16**

115 "I don't use Facebook any more because none of my friends use it, so there's no point," says Viktoria. Alina says she uses Snapchat rather than Facebook but doesn't think Facebook is full of old people, just "more middle-aged people, like in their 30s 120 and 40s". The two girls mainly use Snapchat "for everything, messaging, pictures … and WhatsApp for groups from school, to talk about topics we did and projects."

**Emily McClymont, 17, and
125 Cameron Cavens, 18**

Cameron says he tries not to use Facebook because he finds it too intrusive[11]. Emily is also using it less: "I find it a bit boring now. It deals too much with people's lives." However, she says: "I don't think 130 I'd delete it because it's a way of speaking to my family. That's the only reason I keep it." She says Facebook is good if you lose touch with people because you can find them again.

"If all my friends stop using it, I might delete it," 135 says Cameron. He uses Twitter a lot: "I just hate the amount of ads on Facebook. It's become unusable. Twitter is not as bad." Emily also uses Twitter, and that's where she gets most of her news. They also use Instagram and WhatsApp.

140 **Jordan Ranford, 24**

"As soon as the parents got in, they killed it," Jordan says. He no longer has the Facebook app. "I mainly pay attention to what my older sisters are doing or keeping track of things that are funny … I deleted 145 my mum as a friend on Facebook because she was just jarring."

Most people he knows have had Facebook for eight or nine years. Back then it was a way for everyone to upload photos to show what they had been up to, 150 "like WhatsApp but on a bigger scale … and after the parents started getting involved it kind of lost the fun-ness of it, so it started to be a bit sad when you realised: 'Hold up, my mum is posting more than me, like, why?'" Jordan thinks the purpose 155 of Facebook is to feed egos, occasionally to post something with a nice message and for businesses: "It's not what it used to be. There's just so many more advertisements now. It's losing the appeal it used to have." He says he deleted Snapchat 160 when Instagram launched its Stories feature. He mainly uses Instagram, and Twitter is "quite good for political items, which you don't really get on Facebook."

Annotations

[7] to **disseminate** (v) – to spread information or ideas to as many people as possible

[8] to **meddle** (v) – to influence; to deliberately try to influence or change a situation that does not concern you, or that you do not understand

[9] **dodgy** (adj, colloquial) – dishonest or illegal

[10] **monolithic** (adj) – a monolithic organization is very large and powerful and difficult to change

[11] **intrusive** (adj) – affecting someone's private life or interrupting them in an unwanted and annoying way

COMMENT

d) Comment on how an app needs to be designed to appeal to teenage users. Think of aspects like engagement, content, design, motivation, accessibility, functionality etc.

LISTENING

2 📖 **SB p. 90/1**   **Webcode** DSW-73067-05

Social media apps such as Sarahah (cf. pp. 90-91 in your textbook) may invite users to anonymously cyberbully peers or any other person using it. Listen to a news report on surviving cyberbullying by Cronkite News and tick (✔) the correct answers.

a) What are possible effects of cyberbullying according to the news report?
- ❏ Cyberbullying can have an influence on someone's self-esteem and mental health.
- ❏ Cyberbullying can lead to social media fights.
- ❏ Cyberbullies may experience triumphs.
- ❏ Cyberbullying can evoke emotional struggles.

b) During which period of time has Grace Martinez experienced cyberbullying?
- ❏ During the past four years.
- ❏ From kindergarten until eighth grade.
- ❏ Up to her senior year at high school.
- ❏ Eight years during middle school.

c) How did Grace Martinez react towards the cyberbullying?
- ❏ As a bubbly happy-go-lucky person she didn't pay great attention and played it down.
- ❏ She changed her looks pretending to be someone else.
- ❏ She stopped talking, blamed herself, and secluded herself in her bedroom.
- ❏ She self-injured herself to relocate the mental to a real physical pain.

d) What's the name of the app on which Grace Martinez was exposed to cyberbullying?
- ❏ Hate pager
- ❏ Pew
- ❏ Vine
- ❏ Happy-Go-Lucky

e) Which results of a Pew Research study does anchor Bayne Froney state?
- ❏ 69% of US teens have experienced cyberbullying and 44% of those teens have been called offensive names.
- ❏ 59% of US teens have experienced cyberbullying and 42% of those teens have been called offensive names.
- ❏ 42% of US teens have experienced cyberbullying and 59% of those teens have been called offensive names.
- ❏ 59% of US teens have been called offensive names and 42% of those teens have experienced cyberbullying on a regular basis.

f) How does the newly developed BullyBlocker by Arizona State University work?
- ❏ From data-based learning the app detects incidents of bullying and alerts parents.
- ❏ The app identifies and blocks cyberbullies on respective accounts and informs parents.
- ❏ The app collects data from specific teenagers who are known for bullying to take legal actions.
- ❏ From data-based learning the app personalizes accounts to predict and avoid future instances of cyberbullying.

3

g) What do Grace Martinez' parents recommend regarding teen cyberbullying?
- ❑ To encourage children to speak up and stand up when being cyberbullied.
- ❑ To consult professional recourses to prevent cyberbullying before it can start.
- ❑ To have open family conversations to know what is going on.
- ❑ To regularly check a child's smartphone and to use the BullyBlocker app.

h) Grace Martinez has become an ambassador for Speak Up, Stand Up, Save a Life, which is …
- ❑ … a self-help group to find ways to stop bullying.
- ❑ … an annual conference that spreads awareness about bullying and how to stop it.
- ❑ … an organization that aims at preventing cyberbullying and suicide.
- ❑ … a new app allowing to address cyberbullies.

The Truman Show – a dystopian world?

3 📖 **SB p. 92/1**   **Webcode** DSW-73067-06

The movie *The Truman Show* was released in 1998, just a few months before reality TV became widely popular with the first season of *Big Brother* airing on mainstream TV.

a) Watch the trailer of *The Truman Show* to get to know the movie's content. If you want to find out more about the plot, do some online research.

b) **Pair work** Discuss with a partner in how far the movie predicted the future.

c) What are the main similarities and differences between the situation depicted in *The Truman Show* and reality TV formats such as *American Idol* or *Big Brother*?

_____

_____

_____

_____

_____

_____

_____

d) Read the info box on dystopian fiction. In how far can *The Truman Show* be considered a dystopian movie at the time it was released?

Info

Dystopian fiction

Dystopia is the antonym of utopia (a perfect society). A dystopian work offers a nightmarish vision of the future, in which the worst aspects of contemporary life are magnified. The characters are dehumanized, the government is exceedingly oppressive and controlling, technology is an omnipresent force and the individual has to fight for itself. Presenting a worst case scenario, dystopian works challenge readers and viewers to think differently about the current social and / or political situation.

Examples: *The Maze Runner* (James Dashner), *The Hunger Games* (Suzanne Collins), *The Giver* (Lois Lowry)

The future of printed books

1 📖 SB p. 95/2

There is not only concern about the death of the newspaper industry (cf. pp. 95-97 in your textbook). What about printed books in our digital age? Will print endure?

a) Read the following BBC article and outline reasons favoring the disappearance of the written book and reasons against it. Examine how the author, Rachel Nuwer, puts across her arguments stylistically.

b) What is your opinion? Will the written book endure? Discuss.

Are paper books really disappearing?

BBC Future, 25th January 2016
Rachel Nuwer

When Peter James published his novel Host on two floppy disks in 1993, he was ill-prepared for the "venomous backlash" that would follow. Journalists and fellow writers berated and condemned him;
5 one reporter even dragged a PC and a generator out to the beach to demonstrate the ridiculousness of this new form of reading. "I was front-page news of many newspapers around the world, accused of killing the novel," James told pop.edit.lit. "[But] I
10 pointed out that the novel was already dying at an alarming rate without my assistance."
Shortly after Host's debut, James also issued a prediction: that e-books would spike in popularity once they became as easy and enjoyable to read
15 as printed books. What was a novelty in the 90s, in other words, would eventually mature to the point that it threatened traditional books with extinction. Two decades later, James' vision is well on its way to being realised.
20 That e-books have surged[1] in popularity in recent years is not news, but where they are headed – and what effect this will ultimately have on the printed word – is unknown. Are printed books destined to eventually join the ranks of clay tablets,
25 scrolls and typewritten pages, to be displayed in collectors' glass cases with other curious items of the distant past?
And if all of this is so, should we be concerned? Answers to these questions do not come easily. [...]
30 What we do know, according to a survey conducted last year by Pew Research, is that half of American

adults now own a tablet or e-reader, and that three in 10 read an e-book in 2013. Although printed books remain the most popular means of reading,
35 over the past decade e-books have made a valiant[2] effort at catching up.
[...] Despite the hand wringing that Jones' Host – said by some to be the first digital novel – caused in 1993, publishers weren't too concerned. "In
40 1992, I spoke to CEOs at probably five of the seven major publishing companies, and they all said 'This has nothing to do with us. People will never read on screens'," says Robert Stein, founder of the Institute for the Future of the Book and co-founder
45 of Voyager and the Criterion Collection.
In 2007, with Amazon's release of the Kindle, that attitude abruptly changed. Almost immediately, the device began causing palpitations[3] in the publishing industry. "Amazon had the clout[4] to
50 go to publishers and say, 'This is serious. We want your books,'" Shatzkin says. "And because Amazon is Amazon, they also didn't really care as much about profit on every unit sale as they did for lifetime customer value, so they were happy to sell
55 their e-books for cheap."
From 2008 to 2010 e-book sales skyrocketed, jumping up to 1,260%, the New York Times reports. Adding fuel to the e-book fire, Nook debuted, as did the iPad, which was released alongside
60 the iBooks Store. "By that time, the publishing industry had lost all possible ability to regain any initiative and momentum," Stein says. In 2011, as Borders Books declared bankruptcy, e-books' popularity continued to steadily rise – though not
65 exponentially, as it turns out.

Annotations
[1] to **surge** (v) – to suddenly increase, to shoot up
[2] **valiant** (adj) – courageous
[3] **palpitations** (n) – when you have palpitations, your heart beats quickly in an irregular way
[4] **clout** (n) – power to influence other people's decisions

For the past two years, there has been a shift. According to the Association of American Publishers, e-book sales, which constitute about 20% of the book-buying market, have plateaued,
70 and Pew's newest data, collected in March and April this year, also corroborates[5] the fact that e-book readership has steadied over the past year. What's more, the Times indicates that the first few months of 2015 actually saw a decline in the
75 number of e-books sold. [...]
While no one can say with certainty what the future holds for paper books, Stein believes that what is a plateau now will, at some point, return to a steep incline. "We're in a transitional period,"
80 he says. "The affordances of screen reading will continuously improve and expand, offering people a reason to switch to screens."
Stein imagines, for example, that future forms of books might be developed not by conventional
85 publishers but by the gaming industry. He also envisions that the distinction between writer and reader will be blurred by a social reading experience in which authors and consumers can digitally interact with each other to discuss any
90 passage, sentence or line. Indeed, his latest project, Social Book, allows members to insert comments directly into digital book texts and is already used by teachers at several high schools and universities to stimulate discussions. [...]
95 Books themselves, however, likely won't disappear entirely, at least not anytime soon. Like woodblock printing, hand-processed film and folk weaving, printed pages may assume an artisanal[6] or aesthetic value. Books meant not to be read but
100 to be looked at – art catalogues or coffee table collections – will likely remain in print form for longer as well. "Print will exist, but it will be in a different realm and will appeal to a very limited audience, like poetry does today," Stein says.
105 "However, the locus of intellectual discourse is going to move away from print." [...]
Shatzkin does believe, however, that the eventual and total demise of print "is inevitable," though such a day won't arrive for perhaps 50 to 100
110 or more years. "It will get harder and harder to understand why anyone would print something that's heavy, hard to ship and not customisable," he says. "I think there will come a point where print just doesn't make a lot of sense. [...]"

115 While some might mourn the aesthetic loss of the printed book, is there anything else we risk forfeiting should print disappear entirely? Some research indicates that there is cause for concern. According to Wolf and others' research findings,
120 electronic reading can negatively impact the way the brain responds to text, including reading comprehension, focus and the ability to maintain attention to details like plot and sequence of events. Research roughly indicates that print falls
125 on one end of the reading spectrum (the most immersive) and that online text occurs at the other end (the most distracting). Kindle reading seems to fall somewhere in the middle. "A lot of people are worried that our ability to enter into the story
130 is changing," Wolf says. "My worry is that we'll have a short-circuited reading brain, excellent for gathering information but not necessarily for forming critical, analytical deep reading skills." [...]
Findings are also mixed for how digital reading
135 affects children. Illustrated children's e-books often include enhancements, including movement, music and sound. But the effect these additions have on reading varies depending on how they are executed. If done well, "they can be a kind of guide
140 for children," says Adriana Bus, a professor at Leiden University in the Netherlands who conducts research into reading, and reading problems.
In several experiments involving more than 400 kindergarteners, Bus and her colleagues found
145 that kids who read animated e-books understood the story better and learned more vocabulary than those who read static ones. [...]
But for all the worries about e-books changing the way we comprehend the written word and interact
150 with one another, Wolf points out that "never before have we had such a democratisation of knowledge made possible." While too much time on devices might mean problems for children and adults in places like Europe and the US, for those in
155 developing countries, they may be a godsend, Wolf says – "the most important mechanism for giving literacy."
In light of this, she hopes that we continue to maintain a "bi-literate" society – one that values
160 both the digital and printed word. [...]

Annotations
[5] to **corroborate** (v) – to back up
[6] **artisanal** (adj) – relating to an artisan, someone who does skilled work, making things with their hands

Mediation

1 📖 SB p. 100/1

You are planning to write a comment for an online round table discussion about the global language of the future. Doing some research, you have come across some information in German about the language "Esperanto". Read the information and write a commentary entry in which you explain what Esperanto is and why you think this language should or should not be the new global language.

Round table discussion:
The global language of the future

Darren9890 says, *"I think, it is unquestionable that English was, is and will be the global language. It is easy to understand, easy to learn and easy to talk! English is a well-recognized lingua franca anyway – from Silicon Valley to science, everyone uses English to communicate their genius thoughts!"*

Nyguen2010 says, *"Considering that more than 1 billion people around the world speak Chinese, it should be more than obvious that any dialect of Chinese has to be the global language of the future."*

You say, …

Was ist Esperanto?

Die internationale Sprache Esperanto ist gemeinsame zweite Sprache von Menschen in über 120 Ländern weltweit. Die Grundlagen dieser völkerverbindenden Sprache wurden 1887 von Ludwik
5 Zamenhof in Warschau veröffentlicht. […]
Esperanto ist relativ schnell erlernbar – etwa in einem Viertel der Zeit, die man für Sprachen wie Englisch oder Spanisch braucht. Die Grundzüge des Esperanto kann man in der Regel bei zwei
10 oder drei Wochenendkursen lernen. Die Sprache hat eine einfach aufgebaute Struktur und sie ist regelmäßig.
Esperanto ist neutraler als andere Sprachen, weil es keinem Land einen besonderen Vorteil gegen-
15 über anderen Ländern bietet. […]

Schnell erlernbar
Esperanto wurde mit der Idee geschaffen, möglichst schnell erlernbar zu sein. Deswegen hat Esperanto eine auf nur sechzehn Grundregeln
20 basierende Grammatik. Es gibt keine unregelmäßigen Verben oder andere Dinge, die Sprachen oft so schwierig machen. Wie leicht Esperanto wirklich ist, hängt natürlich vom Einzelnen ab. Je mehr Vorkenntnisse man durch andere Fremdsprachen
25 hat, desto leichter ist es. Umgekehrt kann Esperanto auch dabei helfen, Fremdsprachen allgemein besser zu verstehen und zu lernen, da man grammatische Prinzipien leichter durchschauen

kann, ohne von unregelmäßigen Formen verwirrt
30 zu werden. […]

Neutraler als andere Sprachen
Esperanto gehört keinem Land, keinem Volk und keinem Kontinent. Man macht einen Schritt hin auf Menschen aus anderen Ländern. Jeder Sprecher
35 verlässt seine eigene muttersprachliche Komfortzone und redet auf einer gemeinsamen Ebene mit anderen. Gleichzeitig betrachten die meisten langjährigen Esperanto-Sprecher die Sprache als Teil ihrer persönlichen Identität. Sie fühlt sich wie eine
40 eigene Sprache an und ist einem oft vertrauter als andere Fremdsprachen. Außerdem beherrschen viele Sprecher Esperanto nach ein paar Jahren besser als die Sprachen, die sie vielleicht in der Schule gelernt haben. Dadurch fühlen sie sich sicherer
45 und reden freier. […]

Wachstum der Esperanto-Sprachgemeinschaft
Nach verschiedenen Schätzungen sprechen heute einige hunderttausend Menschen weltweit die Sprache aktiv. Ein paar Millionen haben Esperanto
50 gelernt. Esperanto verbreitet sich auch in Regionen wie Brasilien, Afrika, Nepal oder China. In den letzten hundert Jahren hat sich die Zahl der Esperanto-Sprecher etwa vertausendfacht. Zum Vergleich: Die Zahl der Englischsprecher hat in diesem Zeitraum
55 etwa um das Zwanzigfache zugenommen. […]

1 📖 **SB p. 110**

a) Fill in the missing words.

word from the WordPool text	synonym(s)	antonym(s)	word from the same word family
homeland	*mother country*	*foreign country*	*land*
			migration
	fought over, controversial		
	(to) emerge		
		producer	
		decrease	
resentment			
		beneficial	
	(to) put at risk		
			pollution

b) Now add context and form idiomatic sentences with the words from the left column.

_____

_____

_____

_____

_____

_____

_____

_____

_____

2 📖 **SB p. 110-111**

Identify the following phonetic transcriptions for words from pp. 110-111 in your textbook. Use your knowledge of other languages to learn new vocabulary more efficiently.

transcription	word	other languages
/dʒɔɪnt/	**joint**	**F: joint (adj), joindre (v)**
/ɪkˈsplɔɪtətɪv/		
/ˌɪntərˈækʃ(ə)n/		
/ədˈvɑːns/		
/maɪˈɡreɪt/		
/ˌpɜː(r)sɪˈkjuːʃ(ə)n/		
/kənˈtestɪd /		
/ˈræpɪd/		
/kəˌlæbəˈreɪʃ(ə)n/		
/rɪˈzɔː(r)s/		

3 📖 **SB p. 110-111**

Complete the text with words from pp. 110-111 in your textbook. The highlighted prepositions can help you find the right expression.

Globalization is, of course, a worldwide _____ and it is highly _____ as it

_____ about many changes and challenges in the long run. When _____

countries and their population are _____, it can only be _____ to

_____. As a consequence, many people harbor _____ against multinational

_____. But implemented justly, globalization also has _____ positive

_____. International _____ undermines xenophobia and isolationism. The

_____ of humanity is at _____. It is urgent to _____ in

time because we're running out of _____.

Analysing a speech

1 📖 **SB p. 113/4** **Webcode** DSW-73067-07

a) Watch the first minute of Greta Thunberg's speech at the UN Climate Action Summit 2019 and read the transcript.

Greta Thunberg's speech at the UN Climate Action Summit 2019

Part 1

My message is that we'll be watching you.

This is all wrong. I shouldn't be up here. I should be back in school on the other side of the ocean. Yet you all come to us young people for hope. How dare you!

You have stolen my dreams and my childhood with your empty words. And yet I'm one of the lucky ones. People are
5 suffering. People are dying. Entire ecosystems are collapsing. We are in the beginning of a mass extinction, and all you can talk about is money and fairy tales of eternal economic growth. How dare you!

(You'll find the rest of the speech on p. 52 in this workbook.)

b) Don't forget that speeches are meant to be presented aloud, that's why the orators have a tremendous impact on the effect of their words. Why is Greta Thunberg's introduction so effective? Fill in the t-chart below.

style / language	Thunberg's presentation techniques

Prepositions

2 📖 **SB p. 112/2**

Even advanced learners of English have difficulty using the right prepositions. Do the following exercise to improve your skills. Fill in the correct prepositions.

Celebrity influence in politics

Should celebrities like Leonardo DiCaprio become involved _____ politics? _____ the one hand, they aren't

experts _____ the field. _____ the other hand, they may still be properly informed _____ governmental

affairs. But when famous personalities decide to participate _____ politics without really understanding it,

there's a significant danger _____ their spreading highly subjective opinions _____ important issues. As a

result, many people argue that stars should just stick _____ their profession.

Some celebrities engage _____ politics to make use _____ their fame _____ order to have a positive

impact _____ society. Other stars, however, just seek to increase their fan base rather than educate the

public. A big significant concern _____ celebrity involvement _____ politics is their level _____ education

_____ a particular subject. Are they really aware _____ all essential aspects _____ a topic or are they

only considering one angle _____ a political issue? If the latter is true, their fans are misled to draw equally

uninformed conclusions _____ significant political matters. Obviously, this would spark opposition _____

real experts like scientists who tend to care more _____ facts than movie stars.

3 **EXTRA**

Comment on the following statement: "Celebrity-meddling in politics does more harm than good."

_____

_____

_____

_____

_____

_____

_____

4 📖 **SB p. 117/2**

a) Now have a closer look at the second part of Greta Thunberg's emotional speech. Read the text intensively and give examples of stylistic and rhetorical devices (cf. p. 115 in your textbook) and their effects. Use the grid below.

Greta Thunberg's speech at the UN Climate Action Summit 2019

Part 2

[...] For more than 30 years, the science has been crystal clear. How dare you continue to look away and come here saying that you're doing enough, when the politics and solutions needed are still nowhere in sight.

5 You say you hear us and that you understand the urgency. But no matter how sad and angry I am, I do not want to believe that. Because if you really understood the situation and still kept on failing to act, then you would be evil. And that I refuse to believe.

10 The popular idea of cutting our emissions in half in 10 years only gives us a 50% chance of staying below 1.5 degrees [Celsius], and the risk of setting off irreversible chain reactions beyond human control.

Fifty percent may be acceptable to you. But those 15 numbers do not include tipping points[1], most feedback loops[2], additional warming hidden by toxic air pollution or the aspects of equity[3] and climate justice. They also rely on my generation sucking hundreds of billions of tons of your CO_2 out of the air with technologies that 20 barely exist.

So a 50% risk is simply not acceptable to us — we who have to live with the consequences.

To have a 67% chance of staying below a 1.5 degree global temperature rise – the best odds[4] given by the 25 [Intergovernmental Panel on Climate Change] – the world had 420 gigatons of CO_2 left to emit back on Jan. 1st, 2018. Today that figure is already down to less than 350 gigatons.

How dare you pretend that this can be solved with just 30 'business as usual' and some technical solutions? With today's emissions levels, that remaining CO_2 budget will be entirely gone within less than 8 1/2 years.

There will not be any solutions or plans presented in line with these figures here today, because these numbers are 35 too uncomfortable. And you are still not mature enough to tell it like it is.

You are failing us. But the young people are starting to understand your betrayal. The eyes of all future generations are upon you. And if you choose to fail us, I 40 say: We will never forgive you.

We will not let you get away with this. Right here, right now is where we draw the line. The world is waking up. And change is coming, whether you like it or not.

Thank you.

Annotations
1 **tipping point** (n) – threshold that, when exceeded, can lead to large changes in the state of a system
2 **feedback loop** (n) – in climate change, a feedback loop is the equivalent of a vicious circle, something that accelerates a warming trend
3 **equity** (n) – fairness, justness
4 **odds** (n) – chance, probability

quote	stylistic / rhetorical device	effect

b) Compare Greta Thunberg's speech to Barack Obama's sober yet equally convincing style (textbook pp. 116-117).

_____

_____

_____

_____

_____

_____

_____

_____

5 **EXTRA**

After the UN Climate Action Summit in 2019, Donald Trump, the former president of the United States and a notorious denier of climate change, publicly mocked Greta Thunberg tweeting that the then 16-year-old climate crisis activist who has inspired protesters worldwide had an "Anger Management problem".

a) Do some online research and try to find Donald Trump's tweets about climate change in general and Greta Thunberg in particular. Take notes.

_____

_____

b) Eleven months later, Greta Thunberg delivered the perfect riposte to Trump's tweet when Trump freaked out because he didn't want to accept his defeat in the presidential election:

"So ridiculous. Donald must work on his Anger Management problem, then go to a good old-fashioned movie with a friend! Chill Donald, Chill!"

Comment on the tweets.

_____

_____

_____

_____

_____

4

We Are the Weather

1 📖 SB p. 119/2

a) In *We Are the Weather: Saving the Planet Begins at Breakfast*, a non-fictional collection of essays about climate change published in 2019, Jonathan Safran Foer claims that individual choices like eating less meat would have a very positive impact if made by many. Read the following text carefully.

Extract

Open your eyes

by Jonathan Safran Foer

[...] We live our lives without making ripples, much less waves. And when it comes to the planetary crisis, many of us feel lost inside the causes and effects, confused by the ever-changing statistics, frustrated by the rhetoric.
5 We feel powerless, yet inexplicably calm. How are we, ordinary civilians, supposed to do anything about a crisis that we know about but don't believe in, that we have a muddled (at best) understanding of, and that we have no obvious ways to combat?
10 Watching Al Gore's *An Inconvenient Truth* was an intellectual and emotional revelation for me. When the screen went dark after the final image, our situation seemed perfectly clear, as did my responsibility to participate in the struggle. Like the tens of thousands of
15 Americans who went straight to their local recruiting offices upon hearing the news of Pearl Harbor, I felt eager to enlist.
And when that film's credits rolled, at the moment of greatest enthusiasm to do whatever was asked to work
20 against the imminent apocalypse that Gore had just delineated for us, suggested actions appeared on the screen. "Are you ready to change the way you live? The climate crisis can be solved. Here's how to start."
Tell your parents not to ruin the world that you will
25 live in. If you are a parent, join with your children to save the world they will live in. Switch to renewable sources of energy. Call your power company to see if they offer green energy. If they don't, ask them why not.

Vote for leaders who pledge to solve this crisis. Write
30 to congress. If they don't listen, run for congress. Plant trees, lots of trees. Speak up in your community. Call radio shows and write newspapers. Insist that America freeze CO2 emissions. Join international efforts to stop global warming. Reduce our dependence on foreign oil;
35 help farmers grow alcohol fuels. Raise fuel economy standards, require lower emissions from automobiles. If you believe in prayer, pray that people will find the strength to change. In the words of an African Proverb, when you pray, move your feet. Encourage everyone you
40 know to see this movie.
I found that list frustratingly vague (Call radio shows and say what exactly, and toward what end?), unproductive (I can tell my parents not to ruin the world I will live in, and they can tell their parents the same, but at some point,
45 doesn't someone have to actually do something?), plainly unrealistic ("Hello, Mr. President, it's me. Sorry I had you on hold – I was just helping some farmers grow alcohol fuels – but now that I have you, I insist that America freeze CO2 emissions") and tautological in a way that
50 would have been laughable if I weren't on the verge of tears (Watch this movie so that you can encourage others to watch this movie so that they can encourage others to watch this movie).
It is good to speak up, good to recycle, to plant trees, lots
55 of trees. [...] According to a 2017 analysis, recycling and tree planting are among the most often recommended personal choices to combat climate change, but they aren't "high impact" – they are feelings more than actions. [...]

COMPREHENSION

b) Outline why "watching Al Gore's *An Inconvenient Truth* was an intellectual and emotional revelation" (ll. 10-11) for the author. Focus on the positive aspects.

_____

_____

_____

_____

_____

ANALYSIS

c) Analyse how the author uses language to get across his frustration with the advice given at the end of the film.

_____

_____

_____

_____

_____

_____

_____

_____

_____

COMMENT

d) Comment on the author's statement "when it comes to the planetary crisis, many of us feel lost inside the causes and effects" (ll. 2-3).

_____

_____

_____

_____

_____

_____

_____

_____

_____

_____

_____

4

Globalization and the fashion industry

1   📖 **SB p. 123/4**

Read the text on p. 123 in your textbook again and fill in the grid.

impact of "fast fashion" on the people	impact on the environment	ways out

2   **EXTRA**

Read the method box. Then describe and analyse the cartoon. Focus on the irony of the situation depicted.

"Whenever I get discouraged, I just say to myself 'Sure, my company exploits indigenous people around the world, plunders natural resources and leaves economic, cultural and environmental desolation in its wake, but, by golly, that's not what defines me as a person!' It works like magic every time!"

Method

Analysing a cartoon

Description: about one third of your text

- Start with the most important elements and be precise, someone who does not know the cartoon must be able to picture it.
- Don't forget to have a closer look at the drawing style.
- Does the action take place on one level only or is there a foreground and a background?
- Is the main action (usually in the center) the only one displayed?

Analysis / interpretation: about two thirds of your text

- Explain the texts in speech bubbles and captions and the context of the cartoon.
- Is the drawing style simple or sophisticated, are the characters and the setting drawn realistically or in a very simply way?
- Look out for exaggerations, symbols that represent larger ideas or concepts, labels on objects that make it clearer what they refer to, analogies and the irony of the situation depicted.
- What is more important to get the cartoon's irony? The drawing or the text? What's the effect like?
- Final step: Comment on the cartoon's message by expressing your personal opinion.

Backlash – globalization and its discontents

1 📖 **SB p. 129/2**

a) Read the article on pp. 127-129 in your textbook again and consider the two quotes below.

> "The EU is not perfect, but it's the best idea we've had so far."
> *Jürgen Klopp, team manager of Liverpool FC*

> "Globalization is a fact, because of technology, because of an integrated global supply chain, because of changes in transportation. And we're not going to be able to build a wall around that."
> *Barack Obama*

b) Find arguments why nationalism as a backlash to globalization won't solve any problems. Note them down in the grid.

	The dangerous effects of nationalism
Politics and peace	
The economy	
The environment	

c) Write a comment or prepare a short speech on one of the two quotes or on the dangers of nationalism.

Writing a comment

PRE-WRITING

1 Group work 📖 SB p. 130/1

The stage in the process of writing in which you produce ideas for the later text is decisive for the quality of your comment. You can use graphic organizers such as mind maps, do research, create word banks on the topic or ask questions to improve your knowledge. Asking and answering questions is more efficient in pair or group work. Do the following exercise to improve your knowledge about globalization.

Milling around: Your class is separated into two groups indicated by badges in two different colours. Walk around in the classroom to meet members of the other group, they will tell you the answer to a question on globalization of their choice. You'll then have to guess the question. Take turns.

Group A	Group B
• What images come to mind when you hear the word 'globalization'? • Has globalization generally improved people's lives? • How long has the term 'globalization' been used? • Do you think it's okay to ignore globalization? • When and how has globalization affected your life? • Which countries profit the most or the least from globalization? • What will globalization look like in the future? • Will globalization make us all the same in the future?	• What exactly is globalization? • Would globalization have happened without the internet? • How would your life be different without globalization? • Living in a global village – dream or nightmare? • Do you think globalization will reduce or increase the social divide? • Do you think globalization could end in a world with just one giant country called the United States of the World? • What do you think indigenous people think about globalization? • Can you measure globalization?

STRUCTURING

2 📖 SB p. 133/5

a) Read the following quotes and decide to which one you can relate best.

> "Globalization is not a monolithic force but an evolving set of consequences – some good, some bad and some unintended. It is the new reality."
> *John B. Larson (American politician and businessman, member of the Democratic Party)*

> "Too often we participate in the globalization of indifference. May we strive instead to live global solidarity."
> *Pope Francis*

> "It has been said that arguing against globalization is like arguing against the laws of gravity."
> *Kofi Annan (former UN Secretary-General)*

b) Prepare a comment on the quote you have chosen. Set up a flow chart or use bullet points to put your ideas and arguments in a logical order. You can use the grid on the next page.

introduction	
thesis statement	
arguments	
conclusion	

WRITING

3 SB p. 133/7

a) Now write a first draft of your comment.

b) Edit your text:
- Use structural vocabulary for smooth transitions.
- Review your sentence structures and the coherence of the paragraphs again.
- Check your text for grammatical correctness and the right choice of words.

Mediation

Texts like "The future of work" (cf. pp. 136-137 in your textbook) offer glimpses of where our society and the working world is heading. In order to predict the future, it is also essential to understand the past. The International Youth Forum has launched a campaign for teenagers called *Understanding Globalization Yesterday, Today and in the Future*. Your task is to contribute a coherent English text on the topic "Guest workers in Europe: 55 years of international encounters" for its website. Summarize the text below to inform fellow students about facts, opportunities and challenges.

Erstes „Gastarbeiter-Abkommen" vor 55 Jahren

Im Dezember 1955 unterzeichneten Deutschland und Italien das erste „Gastarbeiter"-Anwerbeabkommen. Damit kamen italienische Arbeiter nach Deutschland, um den steigenden
5 Bedarf an Arbeitskräften in Zeiten des Wirtschaftsbooms zu decken. Das Abkommen markierte den Beginn für die Einwanderung hunderttausender ausländischer Arbeitnehmer.
Anfang der 1950er-Jahre brummte die Wirtschaft
10 im Nachkriegsdeutschland. Steigende Industrieproduktion und die ersten wehrpflichtigen Jahrgänge ließen die Arbeitslosenzahlen sinken und erhöhten im ganzen Land den Bedarf an Arbeitskräften, insbesondere im landwirtschaftlichen
15 Sektor und im Bergbau. Auch für den Straßen- und Brückenbau wurden händeringend Arbeiter gesucht. Ganz anders in Italien: Vor allem im Süden des Landes waren viele Menschen ohne Beschäftigung.
20 Die wirtschaftliche Situation in Italien und Deutschland veranlasste beide Regierungen zu einer Übereinkunft: Am 20. Dezember 1955 unterzeichneten Bundesarbeitsminister Anton Storch und der italienische Außenminister Martino in Rom
25 das deutsch-italienische Anwerbeabkommen.
Es erlaubte deutschen Unternehmen, dringend benötigte Arbeitskräfte aus Italien zu beschäftigen. Bis heute sind rund vier Millionen Italiener zum Arbeiten nach Deutschland gekommen.
30 Das deutsch-italienische Anwerbeabkommen wurde zudem Vorbild für weitere bilaterale Vereinbarungen: Fünf Jahr später schloss Deutschland mit Spanien und Griechenland ein Doppelabkommen, 1961 folgte die Türkei. 1963 wurde mit Marokko
35 ein Abkommen zur Anwerbung von Arbeitskräften geschlossen, gefolgt von Portugal, Tunesien und Jugoslawien.
[...] Die Praxis der Anwerbeverträge veränderte die

europäischen Migrationsverhältnisse grundlegend
40 und war wegweisend für weitere Migrationsbewegungen in Europa.
Durch die Anwerbeabkommen wuchs die Zahl der ausländischen Beschäftigten in Deutschland von rund 280.000 im Jahr 1960, auf 2,6 Millionen 1973.
45 Die überwiegend männlichen, jungen Angeworbenen wurden vor allem für einfache, körperliche Arbeit im industriellen Gewerbe eingesetzt. Die Arbeiter lebten ohne Familienangehörige in Baracken oder Sammelunterkünften. Weil ihr Aufenthalt nur
50 vorübergehend sein sollte, wurden sie als „Gastbeiter" bezeichnet. Das sogenannte Rotationsprinzip sah vor, dass sie nach Ablauf der Aufenthaltsfrist in ihre Heimatländer zurückkehren und andere an ihre Stelle treten sollten.
55 In der Praxis zeigte sich aber ein anderer Trend. Viele Unternehmen wollten die eingearbeiteten Arbeitskräfte weiter beschäftigen, wodurch sich deren Aufenthalt verlängerte. Ihnen folgten immer öfter auch ihre Familienangehörigen nach Deutsch-
60 land. Der Ausländeranteil an der Wohnbevölkerung in Deutschland wuchs im Zuge der Anwerbepolitik von 1,2 Prozent im Jahr 1960 auf über 4,9 Prozent 1970. [...]
Das System der Arbeitsmigration in Deutschland
65 ist heute stark an den Bedürfnissen des Arbeitsmarktes orientiert: Während der Aufenthalt von Arbeitskräften mit geringer Qualifikation zeitlich streng befristet ist, wird ausländischen Fachkräften mit guter beruflicher Qualifikation in der Regel ein
70 Daueraufenthalt in Perspektive gestellt.
Im Rahmen einer EU-Richtlinie wurde für hochqualifizierte Arbeitnehmer die sogenannte Blue Card-Regelung beschlossen: Ähnlich wie die Green Card in den USA, soll mit ihr auch ein längerer Aufent-
75 halt gestattet werden. [...]

Speaking

MONOLOGUE

1  **SB p. 142/5**

Pair work One of you works on topic 1, the other one on topic 2. Make your statements. Then give each other feedback.

Topic 1:

Talk about the picture and the problems refugees and immigrants are facing when they try to enter the European Union.

Topic 2:

Talk about the picture. What can be done to reduce plastic waste?

DIALOGUE

2 **SB p. 143/6**

Pair work Choose one of these statements and discuss it with your partner.

1   There should be a general tax on plastic to fight the pollution of the oceans.
2   Domestic flights from one German city to the other should be banned.
3   Migration is not a crime.
4   Germany needs more immigrants.

1 📖 SB p. 152

Match the following definitions to the right terms.

	definition		term
1	belonging to the middle class; sometimes used in a disapproving way	A	distinction
2	the leader of a country, for example a king or queen or a president	B	heritage
3	the basic collection of laws which includes the citizens' rights and duties	C	contribution
4	a country's common collection of traditions which are passed on from generation to generation	D	head of state
5	the group of people in a country who have the right to vote in an election	E	constitution
6	a person's children and their children's children	F	descendants
7	synonym for: difference, contrast, differentiation, disparity	G	electorate
8	the share that you give in order to help produce or achieve something together with other people	H	bourgeois

1	2	3	4	5	6	7	8

2 📖 SB p. 152

Fill in the gaps with the right words.

residence | head of state | monarchy | effort | sovereignty | (to) appoint | concern | (to) grant | valued | unjust | constitutional monarchy

One of the last monarchies in Europe

At first glance, the United Kingdom may seem politically backward: whereas in most European countries the citizens successfully fought for the abolition of their kings and queens after World War I, the British have kept their _____ and it has a more than 1000-year-old tradition. Naturally, over the years it has developed into a _____. This means there is a constitution which defines _____ lies in the hands of a parliament that elects the Prime Minister and his or her cabinet. The _____, however, is the monarch. He or she _____ the Prime Minister and opens the parliament. The monarch is highly _____ by most people, though a high percentage believe the monarchy is out-of-date. Many consider it _____ that the monarch is _____ a certain amount of money from the taxpayer (Sovereign Grant). Most of it is spent on the many _____, like Buckingham Palace or Windsor Castle. One of the biggest _____ of the Royal Family today is PR (public relations) and a lot of _____ is put into making sure the public regards the royals positively.

3 📖 **SB p. 152**

Fill in the gaps with the words from the box.

> representative | veto | appoints | opens | consent | presides over |
> signs bills | electorate | votes for | head of state

Role of the British monarch

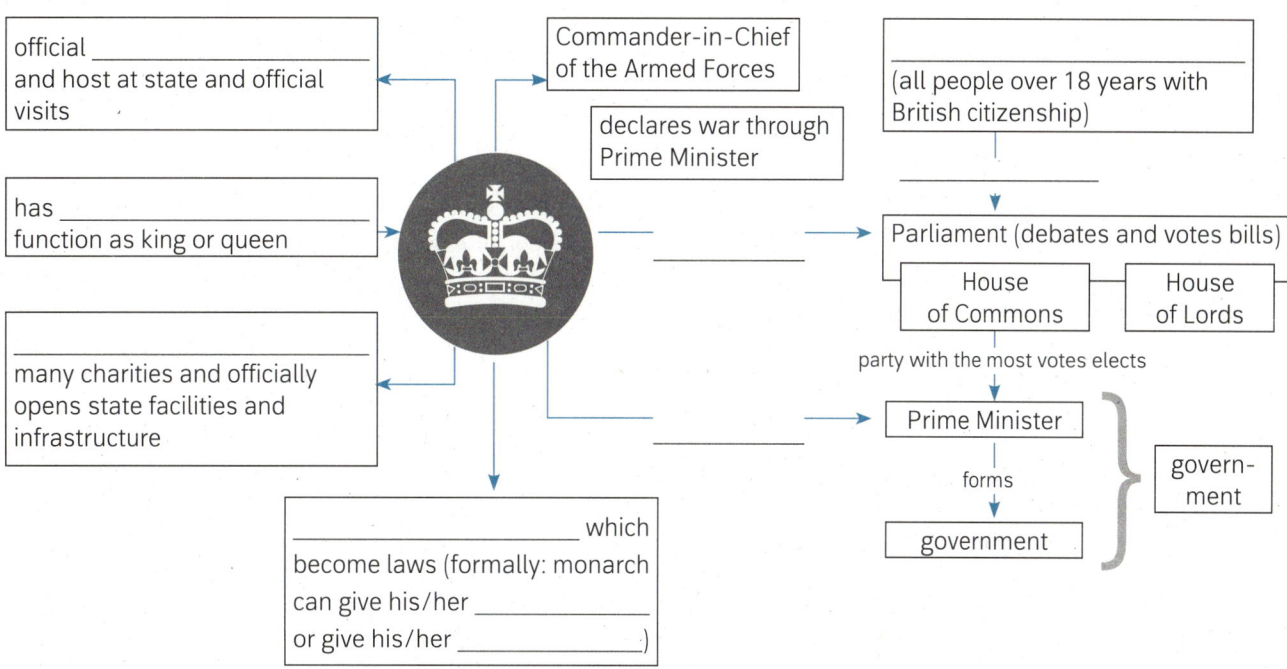

official _____
and host at state and official
visits

has _____
function as king or queen

_____
many charities and officially
opens state facilities and
infrastructure

Commander-in-Chief
of the Armed Forces

declares war through
Prime Minister

_____
become laws (formally: monarch
can give his/her _____
or give his/her _____.)

_____
(all people over 18 years with
British citizenship)

_____

Parliament (debates and votes bills)

| House of Commons | House of Lords |

party with the most votes elects

Prime Minister

forms

government

} govern-
ment

4 📖 **SB p. 152**

Finish the sentences (more than one answer may be possible). Use p. 152 in your textbook for help.

1. The British Isles consist of the countries _____

2. Only the northern part of Ireland, however, is part of the _____

3. British identity is about fluidity and flexibility, which means _____

_____

4. Although the monarch is the head of state and has a lot of important duties, _____

_____

5. Throughout the centuries, the British Isles were subject to invasions from different countries and realms such

as _____

6. British society is often considered as an open one in which _____

_____

7. Even today, classes play a considerable role in Britain, which _____

_____

5

Analysing a newspaper article

PRE-READING

1 📖 **SB p. 154/1**

A headline (and subheading) is supposed to raise the potential reader's interest and make them curious. Normally, it gives a preview of what the article is about. Depending on the type of newspaper, headlines and subheadings can differ substantially. Whereas a **broadsheet** (i.e. quality press) would rather have a down-to-earth tone and tend for a more neutral article, a **tabloid** (i.e. popular press) would rather dramatize a controversy and openly take position. Often, the heading names a controversy or raises a question.

Sort the following headlines into the grid below and say whether they are from a broadsheet or a tabloid. Give reasons.

Info

In January 2020, the Duke and Duchess of Sussex, (Prince) Harry and former actress Meghan Markle, announced they would step back from their official roles of the royal family. Megxit is an informal noun which is put together of the words Meghan and exit. It is a play on words and refers to Brexit.

1

Prince Harry and Meghan to step back from royal family
Duke and Duchess of Sussex say they intend to 'work to become financially independent'

2

PETULANT PRINCE Queen feels 'monumentally let down' by Meghan Markle & Prince Harry who is 'behaving like a teenager', insider claims

3

Queen upset as Prince Harry and Meghan step back as senior royals
Cool reaction from royals as move makes headlines across the Atlantic

4

Exclusive: Palace bombshell
Megxit
Civil war as Harry & Meg quit the Royals Queen sad ... Charles and Wills furious

5

Will Prince Harry and Meghan Markle's daughter have a royal title?
With disagreement surrounding Archie's title, will the same rules apply to the Duke and Duchesss of Sussexes' second child?

broadsheet heading	tabloid heading

2 📖 **SB p. 157/1**

Now read the headline and the subheading of the article below and speculate on …

a) the direction the article is going to take.

_____

_____

_____

_____

b) the arguments the author might come up with to support his or her opinion.

_____

_____

_____

c) possible rhetorical devices that the author might use.

_____

_____

_____

Info

Brexit

The United Kingdom European Union membership referendum from 23 June 2016 was the question whether the UK should remain a member of the EU or leave it. Brexit (a word play made up of Britain and exit) was decided upon with a slight majority of 51.9% being in favour of out.

EDITORIAL   The Guardian, 31 Dec 2020

The Guardian view of Brexit: a tragic national error

Britain is now out of the EU. But this is a day of sadness, not of glory, for we shall always be part of Europe

"And the answer is – we're out." Four and a half years have passed since the BBC's [journalist] David Dimbleby pronounced the result of Britain's EU referendum. At 11pm on 31 December, his words became finally and fatefully true. The United Kingdom is now no longer part of the European Union or subject to its rules. We have closed the door and walked away. We are on our own. We're out.

For many in Britain, it is a glorious day. Departure from the EU, for those who wanted it, is a moment of independence regained, sovereignty reclaimed, and of taking back control. They hope it will sweep the European argument out of British life. They want it to be, in the prime minister's words, "a new chapter in our national story", the fulfilment of "the sovereign wish of the British people to live under their own laws, made by their own elected parliament".

For others, 1 January is simply a moment of relief. The Brexit wars have lasted eight long years, from the moment David Cameron[1] committed the Conservatives to a referendum in January 2013. Even Brexit's eclipse[2] by Covid in 2020 could not prevent Europe's return to the headlines as 2021 approached and the possibility of a no-deal departure again loomed[3]. On this, both Boris Johnson[4] and Keir Starmer[5] spoke as one on Wednesday. These arguments, they both said, are over.

In one sense, they are right. Political parties must look forward, not back. In another sense they are profoundly[6] wrong. This is a day of sadness. Britain's departure remains a tragic national error. We have expelled ourselves from a union that was good for this country and the world. The role of the anti-European press in making this happen was decisive, so it is somehow fitting that a government

Annotations
[1] **David Cameron** – Prime Minister 2010–2016
[2] **eclipse** (n) – darkening
[3] to **loom** (v) – sich abzeichnen
[4] **Boris Johnson** – Prime Minister since 2019
[5] **Keir Starmer** – leader of the opposition since 2020
[6] **profoundly** (adv) – highly, seriously

Annotations

⁷ to **magic away** (v) – to magically remove

⁸ **verdict** (n) – Urteil

⁹ **EU 27** – the 27 EU member states

¹⁰ **UK 4** – the 4 states of the United Kingdom

¹¹ **gloating** (adj) – sich hämisch freuend, mit Schadenfreude

¹² **Tory benches** – the benches in parliament on which members of the Tory party sit

¹³ **Theresa May** – Prime Minister 2016–2019

¹⁴ to **indulge** (v) – frönen, in etw. schwelgen

¹⁵ **regulatory alignment** (n) – Anpassung neuer Reglementierungen

¹⁶ **raft** (n) – Floß

¹⁷ **in perpetuity** (adv) – forever

led by journalists has slammed the door. But at least the EU can no longer be blamed for our continuing tensions, inequalities and failures of governance.

These tensions cannot be magicked away[7]. Brexit was opposed by majorities in Scotland, Northern Ireland, and London and other cities, as well as by most young people and most graduates. None of that is going to change, whatever the overall majority verdict[8] was in 2016 and however tired of the argument we all may be. This is a country divided over Europe. We were divided in the past and we will be divided in the future. Getting Brexit done is a fantasy. It is a supposed solution that only creates new historic problems.

In 2016, many of the most fanatical Brexiters hoped the UK's departure would trigger the EU's breakup. Yet two of the most striking consequences of the vote were the unity of the EU27[9] in the face of Brexit compared with the growing disunity of the UK4[10] over the issue. The breakup of Britain rather than the EU is now the more likely prospect. It would be a terrible price to pay. But the delusions that fed and fostered Brexit still have much of the Conservative party and press in their grip, as a number of gloating[11] speeches from the Tory benches[12] on Wednesday indicated.

Theresa May's[13] warning from those benches posed a far more real question. We must never allow ourselves to think that sovereignty means isolationism or exceptionalism, said Mrs May. We live in an interconnected world, she added. In some ways Mr Johnson seems to understand this. His Commons speech spoke of Britain as "the best friend and ally the EU could have", which perhaps marked a change of tone. But the movement he leads is not interested in alliances or compromises. It feeds off fantasies of greatness, which Mr Johnson constantly indulges[14]. It fatally confuses sovereignty with power.

Brexit is done – but it is not over. In the medium term it leaves behind all manner of sources of future conflict for British politics. These include the fine print of the agreement [...], new immigration controls, the maintenance of regulatory alignment[15], the status of service industries, fishing, access to databases, defence cooperation and, perhaps above all, the ambiguous place of Northern Ireland within the deal. All of these are iterations of a deeper truth: that we shall never cease to be Europeans and will never cease to engage with Europe.

In his novel *The Stone Raft*, the Portuguese writer José Saramago imagines the Iberian peninsula breaking physically away from Europe at the Pyrenees and drifting across the world's oceans in a fruitless search for a new home. Today, Britain can feel a bit like a metaphorical stone raft[16] too. Except that the real Britain will remain anchored in perpetuity[17] across the Channel from the European continent, its peoples, economies and cultures, of which we shall always be part – and to which we hope one day, in some way, to return.

ANALYSIS

3 📖 SB p. 157/2-3

a) Read the article and write down the author's central idea in one sentence.

_____

_____

_____

b) Find five words or expressions that support Brexit (lines 10–19).

_____

_____

c) Find five words or expressions which condemn Brexit (lines 7–9 and lines 31–41).

_____

_____

d) Find two metaphoric expressions and explain their effect on the reader.

_____

_____

_____

e) Find two examples for juxtaposition or antithesis and explain their effect on the reader.

_____

_____

f) Name the protagonists that are in favour of staying in the EU.

_____

_____

g) Name the actual problems the UK has according to the author.

_____

_____

h) Outline the author's train of thought. Use a flow chart like this.

> _The author begins the article by explaining that Brexit has finally been done._ 〉〉 〉〉

COMMENT

4   📖 **SB p. 159/4**

Write an opinion piece with the title _Free at last – with Brexit done, UK freed of foreign rule from Brussels_. Use arguments from the article above, the article on pp. 158-159 in your textbook and the arguments from the box below. You may also do some research on the internet.

> **Tip** You can use the box **Common strategies to make a newspaper article convincing** on p. 70 in this workbook for help.

Five arguments in favour of Brexit

#1 The British people can take back control on all their legislation and regulations, above all the control of immigration (Britain does not have to fulfil certain quotas anymore).

#2 The British economy will do better if Britain can negotiate trade terms on their own as the EU is a customs area which, among other things, protects local agriculture and manufacturing. The UK will, allegedly, be able to have a more direct access to the world market and its (lower) prices.

#3 The members of the EU pay contributions to the EU budget. The last net contributions were about £10 billion which will now be saved.

#4 Brussels slows down decisions with an inflexible bureaucracy. Stupid EU regulations like the shape of a cucumber do not have to be followed anymore.

#5 Few voters have changed their opinion since the 2016 referendum. Still, a slight majority of the voters are in favour of Brexit.

Emphasis

1 📖 **SB p. 160**

After so many years of being an English student you think you know the country? Well, the following trivia about Britain may well be new to you.

For each fact, put emphasis on one sentence with an appropriate way of stressing.

Example: The Scilly Islands are islands 45 km southeast of Land's End, England's most western part. There are 55 islands of which five are inhabited. They have got a very mild climate so that pine trees and palm trees grow there and the water resembles that at the Caribbean.

In fact, they have got a very mild climate so that pine trees and palm trees grow there.

Info

There are different ways of putting emphasis on what you are saying in the English language.

- You can stress the word *while speaking*. Often this is expressed by writing the word in *italics*.
- You can change the word order in the sentence, for example:
  I would never eat insects.
  Insects I would never eat. Or: *Never* would I eat insects.
- You can use the phrase ... *is something / is nothing* ...
  I like football.
  Football *is something* that I like.
- You can put *do* in front of the verb.
  Come in.
  Do come in.
- You can use *really, actually* or *in fact*.
  I appreciate it.
  I *really* appreciate it.
  There is someone.
  There *actually* is someone. Or: *In fact*, there is someone.
- In colloquial English you can use the progressive form to stress something.
  You *are always boasting* about how much money your dad earns.

Trivia about Britain

1. At the Isle of Man TT motorcycle race, motorcyclists ride their bikes just a few metres from the crowd through narrow streets with well over 200 km/h.

_____

_____

2. In Haworth in Yorkshire, there is the 1940s Weekend. At this two-day event, people dress up with clothes from the war, wear uniforms – even of Wehrmacht soldiers – and re-enact WWII.

_____

_____

_____

3. Do you think puffins are exotic animals and can only be found in the Antarctic region? Well, they can be found in Scotland and Northern Ireland too. Puffins in Northern Ireland are an endangered species.

_____

_____

4. Maunsell Sea Forts were built to defend the British coastline from the German *Kriegsmarine* in WWII. Since 1967 one of the forts has been occupied and claimed as the sovereign state principality of *Sealand* by the British micronationalist Paddy Roy Bates.

_____

_____

5. Together with his wife Queen Elizabeth II, Prince Philip has been on state visits in 143 countries. One of those visits has left a deeper impression on the locals: the Prince Philip movement is a religious sect followed by the indigenous people in two villages in Vanuatu. Prince Philip is worshipped as a deity.

_____

_____

6. In the year 40 AD, a Roman expedition was started to conquer the British Islands but it didn't get further than the Channel. Instead of invading Britain, Roman Emperor Caligula had his soldiers collect sea shells on the beaches.

_____

_____

7. In 1962, London Bridge was bought by an American entrepreneur and rebuilt in his hometown in Arizona to attract tourists. Rumour has it he mistook London Bridge with Tower Bridge – which was later denied by buyer and seller.

_____

_____

8. Author Robert Louis Stevenson got the idea for his world-famous adventure novel *Treasure Island* (1883) when his stepson drew a treasure map. Allegedly, looking at it, he immediately wrote down the X that marked the spot of the treasure, named the hills and the surroundings and began writing the back story of the map

_____

_____

Writing an opinion piece

1   📖 **SB p. 170-172**

Look at the photos and read the checklist. Then write an opinion piece on whether it is desirable or not to be part of the royal family. Follow the structure from pp. 170-172 in your textbook.

Balmoral Castle is only one of many royal residences.

The wedding of Prince William and Catherine Middleton took place on 29 April 2011 at Westminster Abbey in London.

Prince Harry talks to wheelchair bound team members as he attends the launch of the UK team for the Invictus Games in 2017. The Invictus Games were originally set up for injured soldiers.

Checklist

Common strategies to make a newspaper article convincing

- ✓ Have a clear thesis or question at the beginning, explain it in the main part and sum up your opinion in the conclusion.
- ✓ Have a clear line of argument: start with a less convincing argument and finish with your strongest argument.
- ✓ Use communicative strategies such as
  - quoting experts or people involved in the topic,
  - giving examples, numbers and statistics,
  - directly addressing the reader.
- ✓ Use rhetorical devices such as
  - metaphoric expressions,
  - a certain choice of words (especially adjectives and adverbs have a huge effect on the reader),
  - including or excluding pronouns.
- ✓ Close the circle: at the end, answer the question you have raised at the beginning of the article.
- ✓ "Take the reader by your hand": lead them through your article. First you should raise your reader's interest. You should keep them reading. Have a good structure that is easy to follow and use paragraphs.
- ✓ Avoid stage directions like "in the following I am going to …".

Some ideas:

in favour of	against
Royals … • have fairy-tale weddings • have butlers • are filthily rich • work for a good cause • …	Royals … • are always in the lime-light • don't have privacy • …

Viewing

PRE-VIEWING

1 · Pair work   📖 SB p. 175/1

Before watching an explainer video called *An introduction to Parliament*, talk about the photo of the House of Commons below. What are your impressions? What are the differences between the British House of Commons and the German *Bundestag*?

WHILE-VIEWING

2 📖 **SB p. 175/1**   Webcode DSW-73067-08

Watch the video once, then complete the following tasks.

a) Watch the video up to **03:50** again and tick the correct sentence endings. Sometimes more than one answer is correct.

The Magna Carta ...
- ❏ allowed British kings to make laws.
- ❏ assured for the first time that no one was above the law.
- ❏ was signed by King John in 1215.
- ❏ enabled a group of barons to vote for a new king.

The House of Commons ...
- ❏ makes proposals for new laws.
- ❏ isn't a part of the British parliament.
- ❏ checks the government's work.
- ❏ is appointed by the monarch.

The House of Lords ...
- ❏ also makes and shapes laws.
- ❏ has almost one hundred members.
- ❏ is made up of people who are selected for their experience and knowledge.
- ❏ only has a ceremonial role.

Select committees ...
- ❏ analyse and closely check the government's policy.
- ❏ take into account what members of the public can say about a certain topic.
- ❏ make recommendations for improvements.
- ❏ don't listen to experts.

b) Watch the sequence from 03:52 to 05:08 again. In your own words shortly explain how a law is made.

_____

_____

_____

_____

_____

c) Watch the sequence from 05:11 to 06:34 again. In your own words shortly explain how elections and voting in the UK work.

_____

_____

_____

_____

_____

3 **EXTRA**

With the help of the online version of the Encyclopedia Britannica and the internet, put the British parties into the right order from politically left to right and write them down in the graphic.

> Labour Party | United Kingdom Independence Party (UKIP) | Conservative Party | Liberal Democrats | Green Party

Political spectrum

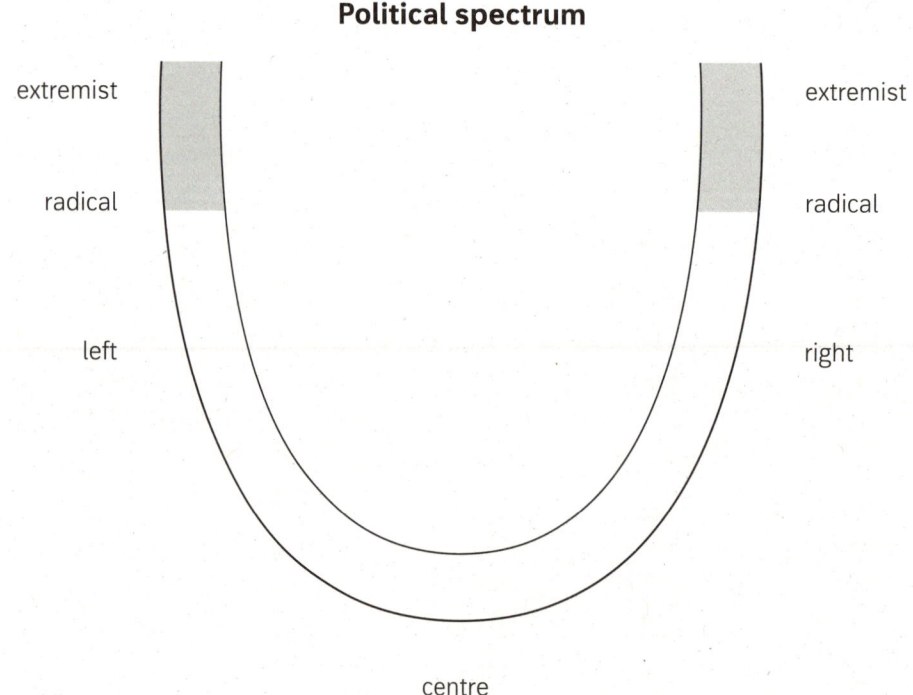

extremist   extremist

radical   radical

left   right

centre

Analysing modern poetry

PRE-READING

1 📖 **SB p. 176/1**

What comes to your mind when you think of "home"? Make a mindmap.

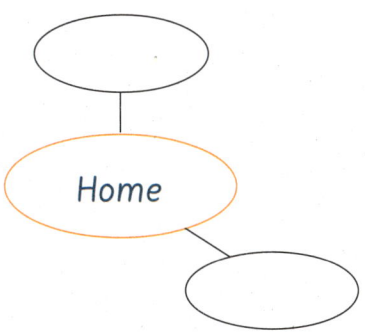

COMPREHENSION

2 📖 **SB p. 176/3**　**Webcode** DSW-73067-09

a) Listen to the poem "Hard Water" by Jean Sprackland. Then read the poem several times (p. 74) and find out about the words you are unfamiliar with.

b) Write down first impressions and ideas about form and content.

_____

_____

_____

_____

c) Fill in the speech bubbles on the next page and write your own ones "talking to" the poem (cf. pp. 176-177 in your textbook).

d) What characteristics does the speaker give her home?

_____

_____

_____

_____

Info

Jean Sprackland is an award-winning poet and professor for creative writing from Burton-on-Trent in the English Midlands. Burton, a town which once played a big role in the industrialization and in the last decades had to undergo a structural change, is known for its hard water that makes it suitable for brewing beer. It is high in dissolved minerals, largely calcium and magnesium. You may have felt the effects of hard water when you have washed your hands or your hair.

Hard Water

by Jean Sprackland

I tried the soft stuff on holiday in Wales,
a **mania** of teadrinking and hairwashing,
excitable soap which never rinsed away,
but I loved coming home to this.

5 **Flat. Straight.** Like the vowels[1],
like the straight talk: *hey up me duck*[2].
I'd run the tap with its swimming-pool smell,
get it cold and anaesthetic. Stand the glass
and let the little fizz of anxiety settle.

10 **Honest** water, bright and not quite clean.
The **frankness** of limestone, of gypsum,
the sour steam of cooling towers,
the alchemical taste of brewing.

On pitiless nights, I had to go for the bus
15 before last orders[3]. I'd turn up my face,
let rain scald[4] my eyelids and lips.
It couldn't lie. Fell thick
with a payload of acid. No salt —
this rain had forgotten the sea.

20 I opened my mouth, speaking nothing
in spite of my book-learning.
I let a different cleverness wash my tongue.
It tasted of work, the **true** taste
of early mornings, the blunt taste
25 of don't get mardy[5], of too bloody deep for me,
fierce **lovely** water that marked me for life
as belonging, regardless.

What is meant by the soft stuff?

What is meant by "this"?

What do swimming-pools smell like?

What may the anxiety be the speaker talks about?

Annotations
[1] Here the Burton accent is referred to.
[2] traditional Burton greeting
[3] **last orders** (n) – the last drinks that customers are allowed to buy just before British pubs close
[4] to **scald** (v) – verbrühen, erhitzen
[5] **mardy** (adj) – Burton expression for moody, sulky

ANALYSIS

3 📖 **SB p. 178/5**

a) Take notes on the speaker.

_____

_____

_____

b) What tone does the poem have?

_____

_____

_____

_____

c) Language and imagery: what is the effect of the nouns and adjectives printed in bold?

_____

_____

_____

_____

d) What can you say about the structure of the poem?

_____

_____

_____

_____

e) What can you say about the poem's sound and rhythm?

_____

_____

_____

4 📖 **SB p. 179/6**

Now write a coherent analysis of the poem. Make use of pp. 178-179 in your textbook.

1 📖 **SB p. 190**

Scan the text on p. 190 in your textbook again. Then tick (✔) the sentence which sums up each of the following paragraphs best.

1 A GREAT NATION

❑ A major distinguishing feature of the USA is its wide range of influence in terms of global politics, e.g. in organizations such as NATO and the United Nations.

❑ The USA not only has a leading role in global politics, economy and military, it is also a big film and entertainment transporter worldwide.

❑ Being a superpower in terms of economy, politics and military, the USA also controls the market of the entertainment industry.

2 AMERICAN WAR OF INDEPENDENCE

❑ The 13 British colonies located on the North American Atlantic coast announced their independence from Great Britain in 1776.

❑ Because the 13 British colonies of the North American Atlantic coast were fed up with foreign control, they put their constitution into force in 1788.

❑ Thomas Jefferson played a leading role defeating the British by writing the Declaration of Independence.

3 A LAND OF IMMIGRANTS

❑ Immigration plays a vital role in the history of the USA, however, more and more migrants enter the country illegally.

❑ Due to the appeal of the so-called *American Dream* to migrants, mostly people coming from Europe, Latin America, India and China immigrate to the United States.

❑ The USA having been a country of immigration for over two centuries, has encountered different waves of immigration, most of them united by the quest for a better life.

4 THE AMERICAN DREAM

❑ The American Dream has remained fairly constant over the decades implying that anybody in the United States can achieve prosperity, success and happiness regardless of their social background.

❑ The American Dream, implying that anybody can achieve prosperity, success and happiness regardless of their social background, cannot be realized by big parts of the American society anymore.

❑ Immigrants are systematically excluded from living the American Dream.

5 AN AMERICAN NIGHTMARE?

❑ In spite of successes in the civil rights movement, America's society keeps being divided in terms of culture, race and class frequently leading to violent clashes between various members of society.

❑ Racism and class-based divisions in American society are mainly prevalent in the southern states due to their former history of slavery.

❑ Antagonistic attitudes towards civil rights have become one of the greatest threats to fundamental American values.

2 📖 **SB p. 190**

Match the definitions (1-12) with the words on the right (a-l).

1	a large number of people arriving at the same time	a	magnanimous
2	a change or addition to the US constitution	b	to resurface
3	a period of ten years	c	to advocate
4	the act of dividing sth into two completely opposing groups	d	abolition
5	to take a long time to disappear	e	influx
6	to publicly support or suggest an idea	f	to linger
7	a long search for sth difficult to find or obtain	g	disillusioned
8	the act of ending an activity officially	h	quest
9	having a lot of influence on sb or sth	i	decade
10	being very kind and generous towards sb you have defeated	j	polarization
11	being disappointed and unhappy because of discovering the truth about sth	k	amendment
12	to appear again after having been absent for some time	l	influential

1	2	3	4	5	6	7	8	9	10	11	12

3 📖 **SB p. 190**

a) Find the odd one out.

1 shortage – insufficiency – surplus – lack
2 to reject – to take up – to adopt – to incorporate
3 contradictory – contrary – opposite – equivalent
4 search – quest – surrender – pursuit
5 advantage – drawback – benefit – help
6 sanctioned – criminal – illegitimate – illegal
7 spread out – widespread – narrow – extended

b) Write a sentence with each word you were not familiar with to show that you understand its meaning.

4 📖 **SB p. 190**

Make as many collocations as possible. Use a dictionary if necessary.

basic	social	powerful	financial
basic idea			

5 📖 **SB p. 190**

Identify the following phonetic transcriptions.

/ˌpəʊləraɪˈzeɪʃ(ə)n/		/prɒˈsperəti/	
/ɪkˈsiːd/		/pə(r)ˈsepʃ(ə)n/	
/ˌɪnfluˈenʃ(ə)l/		/prɪˈdɒmɪnəntli/	

Grammar

Countable and uncountable nouns

6 📖 **SB p. 190**

a) Read the sentences below. Fill in each blank with *a / an* if the referring noun is countable. Leave the blank empty if the noun is used as an uncountable noun.

Info

Remember that in English some nouns refer to things which are treated as separate items which can be counted. They are therefore called **countable nouns** as in the following examples:
a tree, six trees, a city, several big cities, a photo, a box full of photos.
Countable nouns can be singular or plural. They can be used with the article *a/an*, with numbers and many other determiners (e.g. *some, a few, a lot of, these, those*):
New York is famous for a lot of sights.

However, in English grammar, some things are considered a whole or mass. These are called **uncountable nouns**, because they cannot be separated or counted (e.g. *information, advice, news,* but also some substances such as *water, milk* or *rice*):
At the airport, they can give tourists some information about affordable accommodation in San Francisco.

1. Many immigrants to the USA expected to enter _____ land of upward economic mobility.

2. Traditional ideals such as _____ home ownership and _____ financial stability are still popular.

3. The Golden Gate Bridge in San Francisco is made of _____ iron and steel.

4. The US government has _____ new policy on health care.

5. In US culture, the white picket fence has _____ iconic status symbolizing the American Dream.

b) Some nouns can be both countable and uncountable depending on the context they are used in. Explain how the meaning of the word *people* changes in the following sentences by translating them.

1. The American people are said to be quite superficial.

_____

2. The Sioux are an indigenous people of the United States.

_____

Analysing a cartoon

1 📖 **SB p. 195/1**

Prepare an analysis of the cartoon on the right by
following steps a-d. Take notes first.

a) Study the cartoon carefully by first describing it.

"I'd like to keep my gun on."

_____

_____

_____

_____

_____

_____

_____

b) Analyse the characters and objects shown in the cartoon.

_____

_____

_____

c) Explain the message of the cartoonist.

_____

_____

_____

d) Comment on the message of the cartoon.

_____

_____

_____

2 📖 **SB p. 195/2**

Now write a full analysis of the cartoon.

3 **EXTRA**

Discuss the connection between the founding history of the United States and the American self-perception
of acquiring and possessing weapons.

Listening

1 📖 **SB p. 206/1**

a) From what you have learned so far, what does racism mean and imply? Write an acrostic using the letters as initials or placing them in the middle of a word or sentence.

R	_____
A	_____
C	_____
I	_____
S	_____
M	_____

b) Share your acrostics in class.

LISTENING

2 📖 **SB p. 206/2** [Webcode] DSW-73067-10

Listen twice to a radio interview on Cleveland's decision to rename their baseball team, formerly known as "the Indians". Read the questions before listening to the clip for the first time. While listening, fill in the information. You do not need to write complete sentences.

a	The last season Cleveland's baseball team will be known as the "Indians":	
b	What Native American groups have called the team's nickname:	
c	How Sundance, a Muskogee person who is the executive director of the Cleveland American Indian Movement (AIM), feels about the name change:	
d	How long Cleveland AIM has been working towards the name change:	

e	Why it took so long for Cleveland to abandon the name, according to Sundance:	
f	How Sundance describes his own people:	
g	How fans of Cleveland's team have reacted to the initiative to change the name:	
h	How Sundance's group approaches fans with their work:	
i	What Sundance says about fans that are against the name change:	
j	What other professional teams in cities such as Washington have in common with the one in Cleveland:	
k	What Sundance says about secondary schools in Ohio:	

POST-LISTENING

3 📖 **SB p. 207/4**

In the interview Sundance says, "Our issue really is with institutional racism".

a) Use the internet to find out about institutional racism.

_____

_____

_____

b) Explain the statement.

_____

_____

_____

_____

_____

c) In class, discuss whether institutional racism can also be found in German society.

Gun culture

1   📖 **SB p. 211**

a) Read the text below. Outline the main impacts of gun violence on children's and teenagers' daily lives according to the VPC.

Info

The VPC

The Violence Policy Center (VPC) aims to stop gun death and injury in the United States through research, education, advocacy, and collaboration. It considers gun violence not only a crime problem but a public health epidemic. The VPC believes gun violence can be reduced by "applying the decades-long lessons of public health injury prevention and consumer product safety regulation to the gun industry and its products".

"Start Them Young" – The Reality of Children and Guns

Violence Policy Center (VPC), Washington, D.C.   *February 2016*

Much like the tobacco industry before it, the firearms industry – gun and accessory manufacturers, trade associations (both self-proclaimed, such as the NSSF[1], and *de facto*, such as the National Rifle
5 Association) and related publications – consistently denies the risk associated with its products, especially in the marketing of guns to children. As noted earlier, their arguments, such as NSSF's assertion that hunting is safer than bowling, can at
10 times be so divorced from reality that they cross the line from the absurd to the surreal.

Despite the rosy picture painted by the firearms industry, the combination of children and firearms poses risks that are widely recognized. These
15 include death and injury, not just from unintentional shootings, virtually the sole category of firearm death acknowledged by the gun industry, but suicide and homicide[2]. In addition, the exposure to lead[3] that young shooters experience – either when
20 firing a weapon or making their own ammunition, a practice commonly known as "hand loading" – can harm many different body organs and systems, including the brain, and exposure can lead to reduced intelligence as well as behavioral problems.

25 **Youth Gun Deaths**
In 2014, more than 1,300 children under the age of 18 died from firearms: 699 homicides, 532 suicides, 74 unintentional shootings, and 19 from undetermined intent. From 1999 to 2014, nearly 23,000 children
30 under the age of 18 died from guns: 13,756 homicides, 6,903 suicides, 1,723 unintentional shootings, and 395 from undetermined intent.
[...] For the age group one to 17 in 2014, unintentional injury was the leading cause of death, the most
35 common cause of unintentional death being motor vehicle-related deaths (49 percent) and drownings[4] (18 percent). Firearms accounted for two percent of all fatal unintentional injuries. Malignant neoplasms (primarily cancers) were second. Suicide was the
40 third leading cause of death. Guns accounted for 40 percent of these deaths, making firearms the second most popular method of suicide for this age group, behind suffocation[5]. Homicide was the fourth leading cause of death for this age group, with
45 firearms being used in 59 percent of all homicides.
A common myth is that children and teens living in rural[6] areas do not suffer the effects of gun violence experienced by their contemporaries who live in urban environments, despite being exposed to

Annotations
[1] **National Shooting Sports Foundation (NSSF)** – American national trade association for the firearms industry
[2] **homicide** (n) – murder
[3] **lead** (n) – Blei
[4] **drowning** (n) – death caused by being underwater and not being able to breathe
[5] **suffocation** (n) – death caused by not having enough oxygen
[6] **rural** (adj) – in the countryside

50 guns at a young age. The fact is that guns kill rural youth at a rate equal to urban youth but in different circumstances. While more urban youth die from gun homicide, the difference is made up in rural areas through firearm suicide and unintentional
55 deaths. A 2010 study in the *American Journal of Pediatrics* examined all pediatric firearm deaths up to age 19 from 1999 through 2006. The deaths were analyzed by rural-urban settings based on population size and proximity to metropolitan areas.
60 The study concluded:

Children in the most-rural US counties had firearm mortality rates that were statistically indistinguishable from those for children in the most-urban counties. This finding reflects a greater
65 homicide rate in urban counties counterbalanced by greater suicide and unintentional firearm death rates in rural counties.

Parents also have significant ability to prevent youth suicide recognizing that adolescents who commit
70 suicide most often use the family gun. By removing guns from homes where children and teens live, especially depressed adolescents, parents will reduce likelihood of suicide and unintentional death for everyone in the household, but especially for
75 teens.

While 85 percent of suicide attempts with guns are fatal, other means are less lethal: only one percent of cutting or piercing attempts are fatal, while only two percent of poisoning/overdose attempts
80 result in death. Moreover, studies show that many teen suicide attempts are impulsive. Of teens who survived a suicide attempt, one quarter said they thought of suicide just five minutes before making the attempt. There is also little truth to the widely
85 held belief that those who attempt to kill themselves are determined to succeed. In fact, 90 percent of near-lethal suicide attempts do not attempt to kill themselves again.

Lead: The Silent Health Threat from Firearms

90 While the health and safety threats of gun violence can be measured in death and injury, there is another reason guns pose a grave threat to human health and particularly children's health: the toxic lead found in ammunition[7].
95 Lead is a highly toxic metal that is especially harmful to the developing brains of young children. It can harm many different body organs and systems, and exposure can lead to reduced intelligence and many behavioral problems. The federal Centers for
100 Disease Control and Prevention (CDC) maintains there is no safe level of lead in the blood for children, and states, "Even low levels of lead in blood have been shown to affect IQ, ability to pay attention, and academic achievement."
105 [...] For both children and adults, the primary risk of exposure comes from shooting ranges, most notably indoor ranges. At the firing range, children can be exposed to lead through particles suspended in the air or even by eating contaminated[8] food.
110 Even when children do not go to the firing range themselves, they can be contaminated by clothing or accessories from adults returning from the range. The CDC recommends that individuals "shower and change clothes after finishing a task that involves
115 working with lead-based products, such as stained glass, making bullets, or using a firing range."

Yet despite the well-documented public health risk, shooting ranges remain a largely unregulated industry. A recent investigation in the Seattle Times
120 revealed that shooting range owners routinely violate workplace safety laws, resulting in their employees as well as their children and adult customers being exposed to lead. The newspaper found that only 201 of the estimated 6,000 commercial gun ranges
125 in the United States have been inspected within the past decade, but 86 percent of those which had been inspected violated at least one lead-related standard. Thousands more gun ranges are volunteer-led or members-only clubs with no
130 employees, and these do not have to follow federal regulations at all. [...]

As a medical officer for the National Institute for Occupational Safety and Health told the Seattle Times, "Some firing ranges cater to children, they
135 have birthday parties and special events." An NRA official, Susan Recce, told the newspaper, "The issue of lead problems for indoor ranges is extremely rare."

The facts state otherwise. At a Vancouver,
140 Washington shooting range, tests in 2010 found 20 youth and young adults on the Rifle and Pistol Club team had been overexposed to lead. "We weren't

Annotations

[7] **ammunition** (n) – objects that can be shot from a weapon
[8] **contaminated** (adj) – poisonous or not pure

very cautious," one of the participants was quoted as saying. "We would get lead on our hands and eat
145 finger food." Tests showed that the floor of the range had a lead level 993 times that allowed by a federal housing guideline.

There is no cure or treatment for the effects of lead exposure, and the effects are chronic and
150 irreversible. The only option is prevention. And yet, the response from all too many parents is to ignore the threat. In response to an online discussion thread titled "is 3 yrs old too young to help dad clean ar [AR-15 assault rifle]?," one commenter
155 responded:

"The whole lead, chemical paranoia is out of control IMO [in my opinion]. I grew up with lead paint, played with lead toy soldiers, dunked my hands in kerosene[9] while cleaning car parts and used real
160 MEK to degrease stuff. According to my doc I'm in good health aside from high cholesterol. Use common sense. Don't let your kid drink Hoppe's or Frog Lube[10]. Don't let him stick his hands in his mouth … He's more likely to drown or get hurt at the
165 playground than die for touching the bolt of a rifle once a week."

Annotations
[9] **kerosene** (n) – Leuchtpetroleum
[10] **Hoppe's and Frog Lube** – products for cleaning guns

b) Explain the harmfulness of lead in the context of access to arms using the pictorial representation below as well as information from the text.

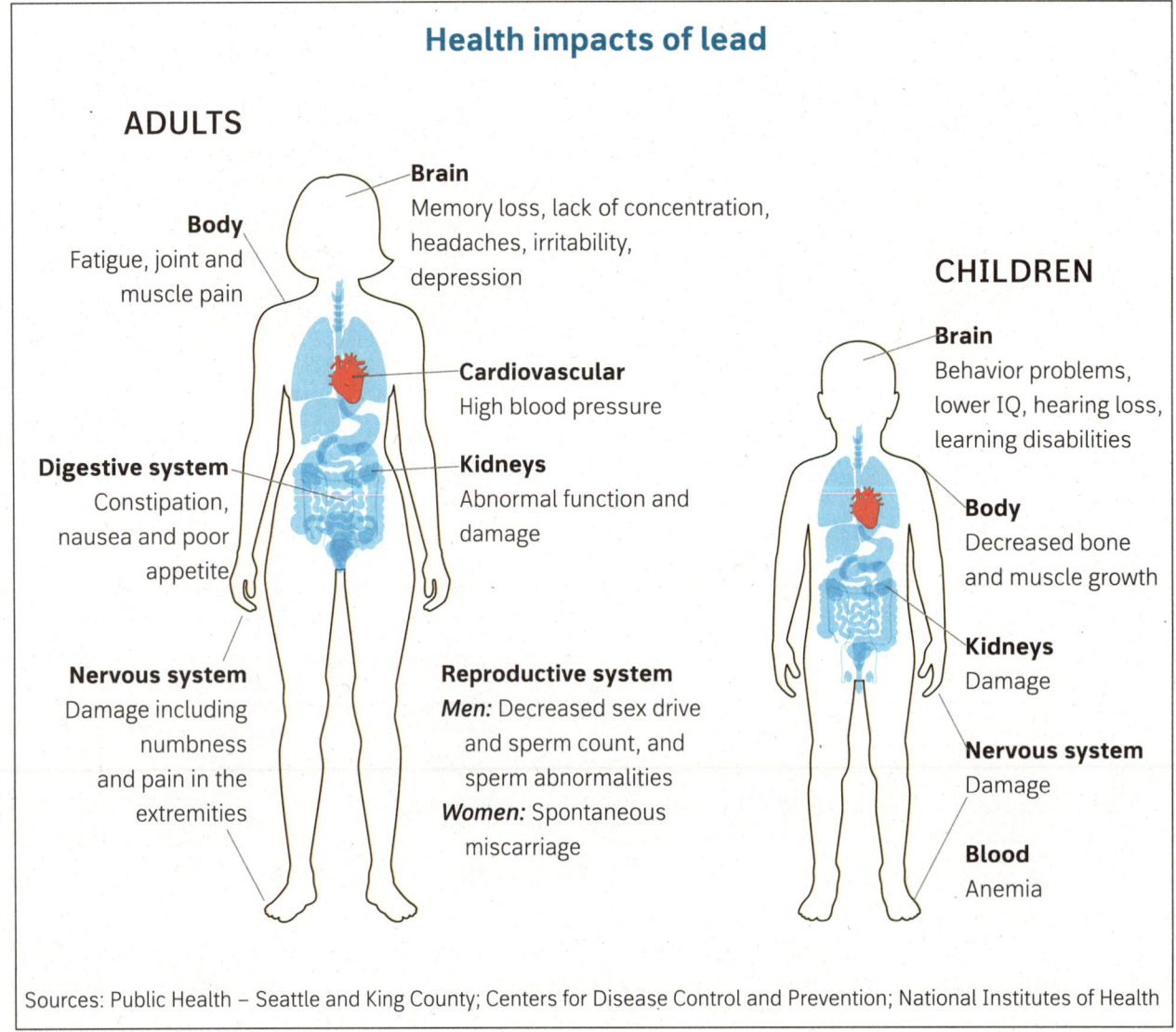

c) Pair work Discuss the commenter's response to the online discussion thread mentioned in the text.

Writing a newspaper article

1 **Pair work** 📖 **SB p. 219**

a) Describe the photo below in detail, paying attention to
- the foreground,
- the background (surroundings),
- the people depicted (their body language, facial expressions, actions),
- striking symbols,
- the atmosphere it conveys.

b) Analyse the emotional impact the photo has on the viewer by taking your detailed description into account.

c) Share your results in class.

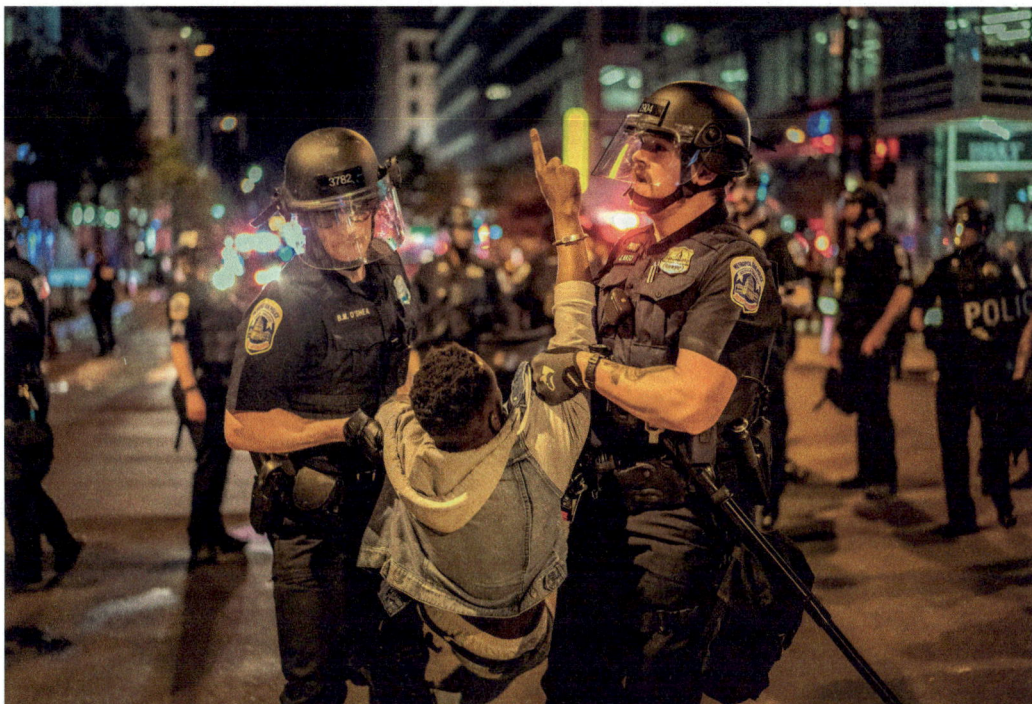

A protester is being taken by policemen. Many protesters gathered in front of the White House in Washington, D.C., on May 30, 2020.

Info

The story behind the picture

Protesters in Washington, D.C., expressing their anger over George Floyd's death at the hands of a Minneapolis police officer converged on the streets around the White House on May 30, 2020. George Perry Floyd Jr. was a 46-year-old African American man killed during an arrest after a store clerk alleged he had used a counterfeit $20 bill in Minneapolis. Film material of the arrest on May 25, 2020 shows a white police officer, Derek Chauvin, kneeling on George Floyd's neck while he was pinned to the floor. Derek Chauvin, 44, has since been charged with murder and has received a sentence of 22.5 years in prison. After Floyd's death, protests against police brutality, especially towards African Americans, quickly spread across the United States and internationally.

2 📖 **SB p. 219**

You are a newspaper journalist who has been assigned to write an article about the picture taken in Washington, D.C., that not only captures the situation but also provides additional information on the racial divisions in American society.

a) Before writing the article, gather more information about the photo and the situation of African-Americans in the United States, especially in terms of police violence. Organize your findings in a mindmap.

b) Now look at the table below providing the general structure of a newspaper article. Match the functions on the right to the general structure on the left.

	general structure		function
1	headline	a	structuring the article by relating to the main idea or topic of the article
2	sub-headlines	b	further development of the main idea, answering further questions (where, when, why, how)
3	paragraphs	c	catching the reader's attention
4	visuals such as photos, pictures, cartoons, graphics, statistics	d	introducing the main idea of the article (answering "what?") and the main subjects ("who?")
5	first paragraph	e	providing proof and illustration
6	following paragraphs	f	providing a structure of the article

1	2	3	4	5	6

Tip You can watch a short video on how to write a news report here:

Webcode DSW-73067-11

c) Every newspaper article also serves the purposes of a content-related dimension. Match the characteristics on the right to the content-related dimension on the left.

	content-related dimension		characteristics
1	information	a	providing sources: • reporting what people said (reported speech, direct speech / quotations) • citing further information, former articles on the topic, academic results
2	language	b	usually past tense
3	tense	c	exact, precise, clear sentence structure, explanation of technical terms to the reader
4	references	d	true, objective, short, punchy, drawing attention

1	2	3	4

d) Write the introductory paragraph, the so-called lead-in.

e) Write the following paragraphs using a clear line of argumentation and providing source references.

f) Choose a title for your article to announce the topic in a short and catchy way.

g) Proofread your article and crosscheck the sources used in the article.

Method

- Think about a fitting layout for your newspaper article.
- If possible, design and typeset your newspaper page on-screen.
- Divide the article into columns.
- Add photos, graphics etc.

3 Group work 📖 **SB p. 219**

a) Start a writing conference in groups of four and correct one another's articles. Assign the following tasks to the different group members:
- correcting and commenting on orthography
- correcting and commenting on structure
- correcting and commenting on coherence (the single parts fitting together in a reasonable way)
- correcting and commenting on providing proof and illustration

b) After having read each group member's article, choose the one you like best to present it in class.

Grammar

Conditional sentences

4 EXTRA

Finish the following conditional sentences. Remember that the condition can either be
- possible and probable (type I),
- less likely or impossible (type II) or
- hypothetical since it was not fulfilled in the past (type III).

1. If the American Dream wasn't beyond the grasp of the working poor,

_____

2. If the firearm industry keeps on expanding,

_____

3. If many settlers had not been persecuted for religious reasons in their home countries,

_____

4. If the illegal status of many Latino immigrants could be ended,

_____

5. "Sonny's Blues" (see p. 219 in your textbook) tells a story about a young African-American man who would

not have been killed by white men if _____.

6. If racism did not exist, the boys' mother in "Sonny's Blues",

_____

7. If the lyrical I in "I, Too" by Langston Hughes (see p. 217 in your textbook) had not been the "darker

brother", _____.

1 📖 **SB p. 228**

Read the definitions and write down the correct words. The transcriptions will help you.

/dəˈmɪnjən/ | /ˌkɒlənaɪˈzeɪʃ(ə)n/ | /ˈtreɪdɪŋ pəʊst/ | /kɑːst/ | /ɪˌmænsɪˈpeɪʃ(ə)n/ | /ˈɑːftə(r)ˌmæθ/ | /ˌpəʊstkəˈləʊniəˌlɪz(ə)m/ | /əˈpreʃ(ə)n/ | /ɪmˈpɪəriəˌlɪz(ə)m/

definition	word
the process of establishing foreign control	
authority, control over a country or region	
the study of the cultural legacy of colonialism	
a hereditary social class in Hindu society	
impact, ramifications	
a small settlement established for trading	
a policy of extending a country's power through colonization	
liberation	
unjust or cruel exercise of power	

2 📖 **SB p. 228**

Complete the crossword with nouns form the WordPool text on p. 228 in your textbook.

DOWN

(1) cruel or unfair treatment of a group of people
(2) a state of latent hostility between people, groups or countries
(3) the state of having paid work
(4) the continuation of trying to do something despite difficulties or opposition

ACROSS

(5) a great difference
(6) violent action organized by a group of people who want to change the political system
(7) a religious person bringing their faith to people in another part of the world
(8) a business or company
(9) the state of having control over people or a situation

Grammar

3 Adjectives and adverbs 📖 SB p. 228

a) Fill in the correct adverbs.

adjective	adverb	adjective	adverb
large	*largely*	massive	
independent		equal	
extreme		crucial	

b) Scan the WordPool text on p. 228 in your textbook and find at least ten adjectives and five adverbs.

_____

_____

_____

_____

Language support

Different types of adverbs
- adverbs of place (e.g. *here, there*)
- adverbs of time (e.g. *today, yesterday, just, still*)
- adverbs of frequency (e.g. *always, usually, never*)
- adverbs of manner (e.g. *carefully, anxiously*)

c) Read the following sentences and put in suitable adjectives or adverbs.

usually | predominantly | always | extreme | unmatched | most important | unwavering | fast-growing | equal | independent | unrivalled | especially | massive | popular | rural | never

1. With the _____ power of its navy, Britain was able to rise to _____

   world domination, _____ in the age of imperialism.

2. India was called Britain's _____ colony, but _____ resistance led

   to a _____ rebellion in 1857.

3. Unfortunately, the _____ tensions between Muslims and Hindus could

   _____ be overcome.

4. Both India and Pakistan are marked by _____ disparities between

   _____ areas and _____ cities.

5. Moreover, women aren't _____ _____.

6. In the 1960s, many colonies became _____.

7. In Nigeria, the north is _____ Muslim. The Christian settlers _____

   stayed in the South.

Writing an interior monologue

1 📖 **SB p. 232/5-6**

a) **Pair work** Before writing an interior monologue for a complex character in a literary work, you can choose a simpler starting point like this one: Work with a partner and prepare a discussion on two of the issues of contemporary India below. Having done research online, discuss what is meant by the key word and elaborate on the topic. Then imagine an individual who is facing this difficult situation at the very moment and try to empathize with him or her. It could be a commuter in overcrowded public transport during the Covid-19 pandemic or a well-educated Dalit who has to do menial jobs because of the caste he belongs to.

caste system	poverty/beggary	child labour	child marriage
Covid-19 pandemic	illiteracy	Kashmir conflict	dowry system
superstition	gender inequality	Sati practice	alcoholism

b) Now write an interior monologue for this character.

_____

_____

_____

_____

_____

_____

_____

_____

_____

_____

c) Now, in a second run-through, choose one of India's strengths and write another interior monologue, this time on your own. Present it to your partner afterwards.

well-educated technology workers, programmers etc.	rapid economic growth	the largest democracy in the world	English is widely used and spoken
a bigger middle class than the U.S. (in total numbers)	Bollywood	cultural treasures	the proud legacy of Gandhi

_____

_____

_____

_____

_____

_____

_____

_____

_____

_____

_____

_____

_____

d) Read the method box below and apply these techniques when writing an interior monologue for Adinah (cf. p. 232 in your textbook).

Method

Advanced creative writing based on a literary text requires more discipline than you might think. Unless the assignment tells you to do otherwise, you have to respect many aspects of the piece of literature to make your text blend seamlessly into the original one:
- Stay in line with the plot and the implicit mood of the text.
- Think of a plausible continuation of the plot.
- The behaviour of the characters shouldn't contradict previous habits.
- Respect register of language, narrative perspective etc.

Analysing characters

1 📖 SB p. 244/4

In the novel *Purple Hibiscus* Chimamanda Ngozi Adichie tells the story of fifteen-year-old Kambili and her older brother Jaja, who lead a privileged life in Nigeria. They live in a beautiful house but their family isn't as perfect as it appears because Kambili's and Jaja's father, Eugene, a wealthy and generous businessman, is fanatically religious and violent at home. In the extract below, Jaja causes a major family scene as he refuses to go to communion on Palm Sunday, an important Catholic feast.

a) Read the extract and use the grid on p. 94 to prepare character analyses of Kambili's father Eugene and her brother Jaja. Use the colour green for examples of direct characterization and the colour blue for indirect characterization. Add evidence / quotes from the text.

Extract

Purple Hibiscus
by Chimamanda Ngozi Adichie

Things started to fall apart at home when my brother, Jaja, did not go to communion and Papa flung his heavy missal[1] across the room and broke the figurines on the étagère. We had just returned from church. [...]

5 Papa always sat in the front pew for Mass, at the end beside the middle aisle, with Mama, Jaja, and me sitting next to him. He was first to receive communion. Most people did not kneel to receive communion at the marble altar, with the blond life-size Virgin Mary mounted nearby, but 10 Papa did. He would hold his eyes shut so hard that his face tightened into a grimace, and then he would stick his tongue out as far as it could go. Afterward, he sat back on his seat and watched the rest of the congregation troop to the altar, palms pressed together and extended, like a 15 saucer held sideways, just as Father Benedict had taught them to do. [...] During his sermons[2], Father Benedict usually referred to the pope, Papa, and Jesus – in that order. He used Papa to illustrate the gospels[3]. "When we let our light shine before men, we are reflecting Christ's 20 Triumphant Entry," he said that Palm Sunday. "Look at Brother Eugene. He could have chosen to be like other Big Men in this country, he could have decided to sit at home and do nothing after the coup[4], to make sure the government did not threaten his businesses. But no, 25 he used the Standard[5] to speak the truth even though it meant the paper lost advertising. Brother Eugene spoke

out for freedom. How many of us have stood up for the truth? How many of us have reflected the Triumphant Entry?"

30 [...] On some Sundays, the congregation[6] listened closely even when Father Benedict talked about things everybody already knew, about Papa making the biggest donations to Peter's pence and St. Vincent de Paul. Or about Papa paying for the cartons of communion wine, for the new 35 ovens at the convent where the Reverend Sisters baked the host, for the new wing to St. Agnes Hospital where Father Benedict gave extreme unction. And I would sit with my knees pressed together, next to Jaja, trying hard to keep my face blank, to keep the pride from showing, 40 because Papa said modesty was very important.

Papa himself would have a blank face when I looked at him, the kind of expression he had in the photo when they did the big story on him after Amnesty World gave him a human rights award. It was the only time he allowed 45 himself to be featured in the paper. His editor, Ade Coker, had insisted on it, saying Papa deserved it, saying Papa was too modest. Mama told me and Jaja; Papa did not tell us such things. That blank look would remain on his face until Father Benedict ended the sermon, until it was time 50 for communion. After Papa took communion, he sat back and watched the congregation walk to the altar and, after Mass, reported to Father Benedict, with concern, when a person missed communion on two successive Sundays. He always encouraged Father Benedict to call and win 55 that person back into the fold; nothing but mortal sin would keep a person away from communion two Sundays in a row.

So when Papa did not see Jaja go to the altar that Palm Sunday when everything changed, he banged his

Annotations

1 **missal** (n) – book containing all that is said or sung at mass during the year
2 **sermon** (n) – talk given by a priest at mass
3 **gospel** (n) – Evangelium
4 **coup** (n) – Staatsstreich
5 **the Standard** – name of a newspaper
6 **congregation** (n) – group of people attending mass

60 leatherbound missal, with the red and green ribbons peeking out, down on the dining table when we got home. The table was glass, heavy glass. It shook, as did the palm fronds on it.

"Jaja, you did not go to communion," Papa said quietly,
65 almost a question.

Jaja stared at the missal on the table as though he were addressing it. "The wafer[7] gives me bad breath."

I stared at Jaja. Had something come loose in his head? Papa insisted we call it the host[8] because "host" came
70 close to capturing the essence, the sacredness, of Christ's body. "Wafer" was too secular, wafer was what one of Papa's factories made – chocolate wafer, banana wafer, what people bought their children to give them a treat better than biscuits.

75 "And the priest keeps touching my mouth and it nauseates[9] me," Jaja said. He knew I was looking at him, that my shocked eyes begged him to seal his mouth, but he did not look at me.

"It is the body of our Lord." Papa's voice was low, very
80 low. His face looked swollen already, with pus-tipped rashes spread across every inch, but it seemed to be swelling even more. "You cannot stop receiving the body of our Lord. It is death, you know that."

"Then I will die." Fear had darkened Jaja's eyes to the
85 color of coal tar, but he looked Papa in the face now. "Then I will die, Papa."

Papa looked around the room quickly, as if searching for proof that something had fallen from the high ceiling, something he had never thought would fall. He picked
90 up the missal and flung it across the room, toward Jaja. It missed Jaja completely, but it hit the glass étagerè, which Mama polished often. It cracked the top shelf, swept the beige, finger-size ceramic figurines of ballet dancers in various contorted postures to the hard floor
95 and then landed after them. Or rather it landed on their many pieces. It lay there, a huge leatherbound missal that contained the readings for all three cycles of the church year.

Jaja did not move. Papa swayed from side to side. I stood
100 at the door, watching them. The ceiling fan spun round and round, and the light bulbs attached to it clinked against one another. Then Mama came in, her rubber slippers making slap-slap sounds on the marble floor. She had changed from her sequined Sunday wrapper
105 and the blouse with puffy sleeves. Now she had a plain tie-dye wrapper tied loosely around her waist and that white T-shirt she wore every other day. It was a souvenir from a spiritual retreat she and Papa had attended; the words GOD IS LOVE crawled over her sagging breasts.
110 She stared at the figurine pieces on the floor and then knelt and started to pick them up with her bare hands.

The silence was broken only by the whir of the ceiling fan as it sliced through the still air. Although our spacious dining room gave way to an even wider living room, I felt
115 suffocated. The off-white walls with the framed photos of Grandfather were narrowing, bearing down on me. Even the glass dining table was moving toward me.

"Nne, ngwa. Go and change," Mama said to me, startling me although her Igbo words were low and calming. In
120 the same breath, without pausing, she said to Papa, "Your tea is getting cold," and to Jaja, "Come and help me, biko." Papa sat down at the table and poured his tea from the china tea set with pink flowers on the edges. I waited for him to ask Jaja and me to take a sip, as he always did. A
125 love sip, he called it, because you shared the little things you loved with the people you loved. Have a love sip, he would say, and Jaja would go first. Then I would hold the cup with both hands and raise it to my lips. One sip. The tea was always too hot, always burned my tongue, and if
130 lunch was something peppery, my raw tongue suffered. But it didn't matter, because I knew that when the tea burned my tongue, it burned Papa's love into me. But Papa didn't say, "Have a love sip"; he didn't say anything as I watched him raise the cup to his lips.
135 Jaja knelt beside Mama, flattened the church bulletin he held into a dustpan, and placed a jagged ceramic piece on it. "Careful, Mama, or those pieces will cut your fingers," he said.

I pulled at one of the cornrows underneath my black
140 church scarf to make sure I was not dreaming. Why were they acting so normal, Jaja and Mama, as if they did not know what had just happened? And why was Papa drinking his tea quietly, as if Jaja had not just talked back to him? Slowly, I turned and headed upstairs to change
145 out of my red Sunday dress. [...]

Annotations
[7] **wafer** (n) – very thin, dry biscuit
[8] **host** (n) – Hostie
[9] to **nauseate** sb (v) – to make sb sick

One way to remember the five methods of characterization is the acronym "PAIRS":
- **P**hysical description (features, clothes, body language)
- **A**ction (referred to as *behaviour* on p. 244 in your textbook)
- **I**nner thoughts (from interior monologues, stream of consciousness or single ideas)
- **R**elationships (reactions to and effects on other characters, mood)
- **S**peech (use of language)

	Papa (Eugene)	Jaja
Physical description		
Action		
Inner thoughts		
Relationships		
Speech		

b) Choose either Eugene or Jaja and write a characterization.

Nigerian poetry

1   📖 **SB p. 248/4**

Below you'll find the first part of the poem "Icarus" by Titilope Sonuga, the author of "Becoming" (cf. p. 248 in your textbook). It broaches the issue of vigilante justice during the aftermaths and turmoil of postcolonialism. In a wave of desperation and brutalization, mobs of violent black youngsters took the law into their own hands and committed horrible crimes like "necklacing", which is the practice of extrajudicial summary execution and torture carried out by forcing a tire with petrol around the victim's chest and arms and setting it on fire. It was used to punish people who were perceived as collaborators with the white settlers in Africa.

a) Go online and listen to a recital of the poem.   **Webcode** DSW-73067-12

b) Describe the reaction of the people who were not directly involved in the crime and try to find an explanation for their behaviour.

c) Identify at least three different stylistic devices the author uses and analyse their effect on the reader / listener.

Icarus
by Titilope Sonuga

I once saw a man on fire
a gasoline soaked rubber tire around his neck
arms flailing like he was trying to fly

I was too young to differentiate horror from spectacle
5 so I asked my mother why
with all the people that surrounded him
nobody brought water

She was navigating a different kind of spectacle
in the bumper to bumper traffic before us
10 she said,

Shhh, don't look at it, we'll be past this soon

and I tried not to look directly at the flames licking at his skin
or the way his mouth froze open without a sound
like an unanswered question

15 Even now
this memory is colored by the normalcy of it
how life went on all around him
this thief
Icarus fallen amongst us
20 This is the way it has always been
we will shield our eyes from the flames
but my country is on fire
every corner of it a smoldering heat
a slow creeping combustion
25 we have flown too close to the sun
with wings made only of feather and wax [...]

Listening

1   📖 **SB p. 251/3**   Webcode **DSW-73067-13**

LISTENING FOR GIST

Listen to a radio interview with Jeta Amata, a film producer who has been involved in the Nigerian movie industry since its beginning 20 years ago.

a) List the three biggest film industries in the world in the correct order (number of films produced).

1. _____

2. _____

3. _____

b) What's Amata's opinion on the term "Nollywood"? Tick (✔) the right answers.
- ❏ He hates it.
- ❏ He loves it because the word was created by a Nigerian.
- ❏ He identifies with it.
- ❏ He's even proud of it.

LISTENING FOR DETAIL

c) Listen again and fill in the missing pieces of information.

1. Expressions used in the interview to describe Amata:

_____

_____

_____

_____

_____

_____

2. More facts about Amata:

_____

_____

_____

_____

_____

3. Common stereotypes about Nigerian films:

_____

_____

_____

_____

_____

4. According to Amata, what's the purpose of Nigerian films and what's not that important?

very important	less important

5. What were the major challenges when producing the transnational movie "Black November"?

_____

_____

_____

_____

_____

_____

_____

Working with a screenplay

PRE-READING

1

From 1948 onwards, many people from the Caribbean came to Britain in order to find work and start a new life. As citizens of the Commonwealth, entry into Britain was easy at first, before immigration rules were tightened in the 1960s. One early immigrant from the Caribbean recalled: "When we came here we swore we were English […]. We were brought up under the colonial rule. […] When you come here, you discovered it's a different thing. If you're English, you have to be white."

Talk about this statement in class. Consider the following questions:

- What expectations of life in Britain did people from the Caribbean possibly have?
- What could their experiences in post-war Britain have been?

THE SETTING

2 **SB p. 255/2**

You are going to read an extract from the play "Small Island", which was adapted by Helen Edmundson in 2019 from the novel (2004) by Andrea Levy (for an extract from the novel, see p. 265 in your textbook). The script of a play is similar to a screenplay in that it consists of dialogue and stage directions (called action lines in the screenplay).

Hortense is a young Jamaican woman, who marries Gilbert, a young Jamaican man she hardly knows, in order to start a new life in London in 1948. In the following scene, she has just arrived at Gilbert's place after he failed to pick her up at the dock.

Read the extract and describe the setting in this scene in one or two sentences.

HORTENSE. What is it you write in your letter? 'I will be at the dockside to meet you. You will see me there, jumping and waving and calling your name with longing in my tone.'

5 **GILBERT.** Hortense, Hortense, let me tell you. I worked a shift at the post office last night. In the morning I went straight to the dock but there was no ship. So they tell me to come back later when the ship will arrive. So I go home to take the opportunity of fixing 10 the place up nice for you …

HORTENSE. Oh, yes. See how nice it is.

GILBERT. And I just lie for a minute and I fall asleep. I so tired. And next thing I know you are ringing the bell and …

15 **HORTENSE.** Do you know what a fool I feel waiting on that dock? Waiting and waiting …

GILBERT. I know …

HORTENSE. And everyone else is meeting people or going off in little twos and threes …

20 **GILBERT.** I'm sorry …

HORTENSE. And then the taxi driver could not understand what I am saying when I tell him this address, and I begin to wonder if this place even …

GILBERT. Sorry. I'm sorry. Hortense, I am glad you are 25 here. Man, I look forward to this day so long.

HORTENSE. (*unconvinced*). Really?

GILBERT. Yes! Of course. I have my wife with me at last.

HORTENSE *is silent.* […]

GILBERT. You wan' a cup of tea? I'll make you a nice cup 30 of English tea. Yes?

She assents with the slightest of nods. GILBERT *goes into the kitchen area and puts the kettle on.*

Take off your coat nah.

HORTENSE *takes off her coat reluctantly. She leaves* 35 *her hat and gloves on. She is wearing the white dress which she wore for the wedding.* GILBERT *goes to her and takes her coat from her. He hangs it over the suit – his wedding suit – on the back of the door.* HORTENSE *is still taking in the room.*

40 **HORTENSE.** Only one bed.

GILBERT. Yes. But nights here very cold, yah know? And we …

HORTENSE. At least you will have a chair to sleep on.

GILBERT *almost protests but decides not to.* HORTENSE 45 *sits down.*

Who is that woman downstairs?

GILBERT. Queenie. She own the house. She is the landlady.

HORTENSE. She married?

50 **GILBERT.** Her husband lost in the war.

HORTENSE. She on her own?

GILBERT. Yes.

HORTENSE. You friendly with her?

GILBERT *freezes and thinks for a moment before* 55 *answering.*

GILBERT. I knew her during the war. She was kind to me. Lucky I remember her address. Lucky she still here. Places hard to come by, especially for coloured boys.

60 HORTENSE. She seem to know all your business.

GILBERT. What? No. She just friendly.

HORTENSE. Who else live in this house?

GILBERT. Winston. Him exactly like Kenneth but honest. And a white woman called Jean. You won't
65 see her much. She work nights.

HORTENSE. She a nurse?

GILBERT. Something like that. Come – I show you how to use the gas ring[1]. It only small but it surprising what you can cook up on it.

70 HORTENSE. I will cook in the kitchen.

   Pause.

GILBERT. This is the kitchen.

HORTENSE. Where?

GILBERT. This ring. This sink. This is the kitchen.

75 HORTENSE. Just this? There is no kitchen down the stairs?

GILBERT. Not for us to use. This is the kitchen. (*Pointing to the table and chairs.*) That is the dining room. I thought you …

80 HORTENSE, *aghast[2], takes this in.*

HORTENSE. And what about the lavatory[3]? Tell me we have our own lavatory.

GILBERT. No. The lavatory is on the ground floor. It's a shared lavatory.

85 HORTENSE. Do you mean to tell me, that every time I need the lavatory, I must go all the way down those stairs and then come all the way back up again?

GILBERT. Yes. (*Suddenly.*) No! No –

   Excited, he goes to the bed and pulls a potty[4] out from
90 *underneath.*

   Sometimes I use this.

Annotations
1 **gas ring** (n) – Gaskocher
2 **aghast** (adj) – shocked
3 **lavatory** (n) – toilet
4 **potty** (n) – Nachttopf
5 to **slop over** (v) – to spill
6 **caan** – can't

He shows it to her. But the potty is full and some of the contents slop over[5] the side. HORTENSE *jumps back in disgust.*

95 Oh!

HORTENSE. Disgusting! What are you doing?!

GILBERT. Sorry! I forgot it was … Oh, no …

HORTENSE. This place is disgusting! How you bring me here?!

100 GILBERT. Hush! [...]

HORTENSE. Get it away from me! I caan[6] believe you bring me here. You live like an animal!

GILBERT. You should see the place I was living when I first arrived – crammed into one room with eight
105 other boys, lying in each other's sweat …

HORTENSE. I don't want to know …

GILBERT. You should see the number of doors I knock on, the faces that cloud at the sight of me. 'The room has gone. The room has gone.' That if they even deign
110 to speak to me. 'If it was just me I'd let you have it, but it's my husband you see, it's my wife you see, it's the neighbours you see, there are *children* in this house you see?'

   GILBERT *strides into the kitchen. He throws the*
115 *contents of the potty into the basin and slams the potty down. There is silence for a moment.*

HORTENSE. What did you just do? There are cups in that basin. You tell me … you tell me you wash your cups in the same place you throw your doings?

120 GILBERT. No. No, I don't. I take it down to the toilet. But you are getting me so …

HORTENSE. You wash in filth! This place is disgusting! You make me come here to live like an animal!

GILBERT. Yes! Yes! And you know what else, Little Miss
125 Stick-up-your-nose-in-the-air, you will have to wash your plate, your vegetable and your backside in that basin too. This room is where you will sleep, eat, cook, dress and write your mummy to tell her how the Mother Country is so fine. And let me tell you this one thing – you are lucky!

THE PLOT

3 📖 **SB p. 257/3**

Summarize what happens in the scene.

ANALYSIS: CHARACTERS

4 📖 **SB p. 258/6-7**

a) Take notes on the characters of Hortense and Gilbert. Draw information from the stage directions and the dialogue.

b) Write a short characterization of either Hortense or Gilbert, using your results from a).

ANALYSIS: CONTRAST

5

It is obvious that expectations and reality of life in Britain as a new immigrant from Jamaica don't match up in this scene. Contrast Hortense's expectations with what reality looks like from what Gilbert tells her and from what she sees. Use quotes from the extract to support your arguments.

WRITING

6 📖 **SB p. 258/10; 261/4**

CHOOSE

Hannah Lowe, a British writer whose father came from Jamaica, once wrote: "In history class, Mr Marsden asked us to write about an interesting member of our family. I wrote what I knew about my father's upbringing in Jamaica, using a word he himself used – anglocentric – to describe his schooling. When my essay was returned, anglocentric was circled in red, and 'No Such Word' written in the margin. I was starting to understand that those in the centre didn't need the language to describe their privilege." Explain what Hannah Lowe means in the last sentence and comment on this statement.

OR

Creative writing At the end of the scene, Gilbert tells Hortense: "This room is where you will [...] write your mummy to tell her how the Mother Country is so fine." Write Hortense's letter to her mother, in which she describes her arrival in London.

Advanced texts **The Windrush Generation Women**

1 📖 **SB p. 265-267**

Read the following article and sum it up in one sentence.

I'm Giving My Thanks To Windrush Women Like My Grandmother This International Women's Day

By Nzinga Cotton, 8 March 2019, Huffpost

[...] This International Women's Day[1] I'm giving thanks to the Windrush Generation Women. They made an invaluable contribution to the social, cultural and economic fabric of Great Britain, but
5 their legacy is at risk of being forgotten.

Windrush Generation is the term given to the half a million immigrants who came to Britain from Caribbean Commonwealth countries between 1948 and 1971. The arrival of 492 Caribbean immigrants
10 on the *Empire Windrush* in 1948 has come to symbolise their landmark journey.

My grandmother made the trip by boat aged 22 from St Kitts[2] in 1955. Like many other Caribbean women she arrived alone, having given up her former life and everything she had known to forge a new one in Britain.

15 She arrived because she was a British citizen and the country desperately needed workers. The British economy of the 1950s and 1960s was still recovering from World War II and the government had called for immigrants from across the Commonwealth to
20 fill widespread labour shortages.

Female Caribbean immigrants played a significant role in the building of modern Britain. As nurses, cleaners, dressmakers and a range of other menial jobs they made a vital contribution to everyday life

Annotations
[1] International Women's Day is celebrated on 8 March
[2] St Kitts is a small island in the Caribbean

in Britain. It's no exaggeration to say the country would not have moved forward in the way it did post-war, without them.

But their lives here were far from easy. Before my grandmother arrived she expected the streets to be paved with gold. West Indian people were taught to expect the very best from the 'Mother Country'. This myth was dispelled as soon as they arrived.

Britain in the post-war years was a hostile place for people with black skin, especially for women. Black Commonwealth immigrants faced widespread racism and discrimination. They were routinely blocked from employment opportunities, excluded from social institutions and given poor housing.

Despite this, the voices of Windrush women have been completely erased from our history. We know very little about their journey here and their day-to-day experiences of life in Britain. The recent passing[3] of *Small Island* author Andrea Levy has highlighted how few depictions there are of the lived experiences of black British women in our art, literature and the media.

There is no public monument dedicated to these women, and in our civic and political life they are largely unremarked upon. Worse, the government has felt entitled to wrongly call the citizenship status of this generation into question.

We all stand to benefit from recognising the contribution of the Windrush generation women.

Celebrating diversity builds empathy and tolerance, and is a key tenet[4] in the fight for social justice.

When my grandmother passed away more than ten years ago I felt bitterly angry that so little is known about the life of women like her. Women who look like me.

Now that many Windrush women are reaching their 70s and 80s we are at risk of losing their stories altogether.

My grandmother never returned to St Kitts. She spent the rest of her life living and working in this country. She had made it her home.

The story of my grandmother's life is central to the story of the British Empire. But it's a story that is rarely told. This International Women's Day, it's time for that to change.

Annotations
[3] **passing** (n)– death
[4] **tenet** (n) – principle

2

Write down the reasons why, according to the author Nzinga Cotton, women like her grandmother should be remembered in Britain today.

3

"The story of my grandmother's life is central to the story of the British Empire." Comment on this statement by considering the information in the article and what you have learned about the British Empire in class.

1 📖 **SB p. 270**

Find synonyms for the following words. They can all be found in the WordPool text on p. 270 in your textbook.

(to) identify		(to) disclose	
work		life span	
feelings		peers	
(to) produce		leading character	

2 📖 **SB p. 270**

Find the opposites of the following words in the text. Use a dictionary for help if necessary.

1 innocence	_____	5 short	_____
2 success	_____	6 unproductive	_____
3 hero	_____	7 boring, dull	_____
4 laziness, aversion	_____	8 inarticulateness	_____

3 📖 **SB p. 270**

Many words are often used in a particular combination called collocation. Find the collocations by combining 1-10 with A-J. In some cases, you will need to insert *of*.

1	tragic		A	love
2	complicated		B	device
3	successive		C	effect
4	dramatic		D	work
5	source	**(of)**	E	verse
6	literary		F	flaw
7	Greek		G	generations
8	stylistic		H	disorder
9	romantic		I	tragedy
10	blank		J	plot

1 _____
2 _____
3 _____
4 _____
5 _____
6 _____
7 _____
8 _____
9 _____
10 _____

4 📖 **SB p. 270**

Find the odd one out.

1 costumes – props – screen – stage
2 jokes – seriousness – puns – witticism
3 pious – blasphemous – insulting – profane
4 demise – downfall – failure – accomplishment
5 sin – innocence – guilt – culpability

Analysing a Shakespearean sonnet

PRE-READING

1 📖 **SB p. 274/1**

Before reading the sonnet below, choose the picture that you think expresses the feeling of loneliness best. Explain your choice.

COMPREHENSION

2 📖 **SB p. 274/2** **Webcode** DSW-73067-14

a) Listen to a recital of Sonnet 97 and talk about your first impressions in class.

b) **Group work** Sum up what the poem is about.

c) **Group work** Paraphrase and examine the sonnet line by line.

Sonnet 97

How like a winter hath[1] my absence been
From thee[2], the pleasure of the fleeting[3] year!
What freezings[4] have I felt, what dark days seen!
What old December's bareness[5] everywhere!
5 And yet this time remov'd was summer's time,
The teeming[6] autumn, big with rich increase[7],
Bearing the wanton burthen of the prime[8],
Like widow'd wombs after their lords' decease:
Yet this abundant issue[9] seem'd to me
10 But hope of orphans and unfather'd fruit;
For summer and his pleasures wait on thee[10],
And thou away, the very birds are mute;
Or if they sing, 'tis with so dull a cheer[11]
That leaves look pale, dreading the winter's near.

Annotations
[1] **hath** – has
[2] **thee** – you
[3] **fleeting** – quickly passing
[4] **freezings** – dark and cold days
[5] **bareness** – emptiness, bleakness, nakedness
[6] **teeming** – prolific, overfull
[7] **rich increase** – plentiful harvest
[8] **wanton burthen of the prime** – lustful birth of spring
[9] **abundant issue** – *here:* child
[10] **on thee** – for you
[11] **with so dull a cheer** – so listlessly

ANALYSIS

3 📖 **SB p. 275/5**

a) Analyse the stylistic devices used in the sonnet (see textbook p. 275 and p. 347 for help).

_____

_____

_____

_____

_____

_____

b) Explain how the images used in the sonnet refer to the feeling of the speaker.

_____

_____

_____

_____

_____

c) Present your findings in class.

4 **Shakespeare's language** 📖 **SB p. 274/3**

CHALLENGE Match the Early Modern English words on the left to the corresponding Modern English words on the right.

	Early Modern English		Modern English
1	ye	a	(you) are
2	woo	b	blind
3	silly	c	kinsman
4	prime	d	brown
5	naught	e	enemy
6	bisson	f	goes
7	twain	g	you (plural or singular; used to address someone you respect)

	Early Modern English		Modern English
8	foe	h	worked
9	art	i	(to) court
10	wilt	j	two
11	misadventured	k	innocent
12	cousin	l	spring
13	goeth	m	will
14	dun	n	unfortunate
15	proper	o	nothing
16	wrought	p	handsome

1	2	3	4	5	6	7	8	9	10	11	12	13	14	15	16

Working with Shakespearean drama

PRE-READING

1 📖 **SB p. 286/1**

Look at this picture from a production of the play *A Midsummer Night's Dream*. What could the plot be about? Make predictions.

2 **Pair work** 📖 **SB p. 286/1** | **Webcode** DSW-73067-15

a) Watch or read a plot summary of *A Midsummer Night's Dream* online. Note down the most important information about the plot and the characters.

b) Compare the information with your predictions from task 1.

COMPREHENSION

3 **Pair work** 📖 **SB p. 286/2**

a) Read the extract from the first scene of *A Midsummer Night's Dream* and sum up the plot.

b) Note down what we get to know about the characters introduced in this scene.

Act I, SCENE I. Athens. The palace of THESEUS.
Enter THESEUS, HIPPOLYTA, PHILOSTRATE, and
Attendants

THESEUS. Now, fair Hippolyta, our nuptial hour
5 Draws on apace[1]; four happy days bring in
Another moon: but, O, methinks, how slow
This old moon wanes[2]! she lingers my desires,
[...]
HIPPOLYTA. Four days will quickly steep themselves
10 in[3] night;
Four nights will quickly dream away the time;
And then the moon, like to a silver bow
New-bent in heaven, shall behold the night
Of our solemnities[4].
15 [...]
Exit **PHILOSTRATE**
THESEUS. Hippolyta, I woo'd thee[5] with my sword,
And won thy love, doing thee injuries;
But I will wed thee in another key,
20 With pomp, with triumph and with revelling[6].
Enter **EGEUS, HERMIA, LYSANDER,** *and*
    DEMETRIUS
EGEUS. Happy be Theseus, our renowned duke!
THESEUS. Thanks, good Egeus: what's the news with
25   thee?
EGEUS. Full of vexation[7] come I, with complaint
Against my child, my daughter Hermia.

Stand forth, Demetrius. My noble lord,
This man hath my consent to marry her.
30 Stand forth, Lysander: and my gracious duke,
This man hath bewitch'd the bosom of my child[8];
Thou, thou, Lysander, thou hast given her rhymes,
And interchanged love-tokens with my child:
Thou hast by moonlight at her window sung,
35 [...]
Be it so she will not here before your grace
Consent to marry with Demetrius,
[...]
THESEUS. What say you, Hermia? be advised fair maid:
40 To you your father should be as a god;
One that composed your beauties[9], yea, and one
To whom you are but as a form in wax
By him imprinted[10] and within his power
To leave the figure or disfigure it.
45 Demetrius is a worthy gentleman.
HERMIA. So is Lysander.
THESEUS. In himself he is;
But in this kind, wanting your father's voice[11],
The other must be held the worthier.
50 **HERMIA.** I would[12] my father look'd but with my eyes.
THESEUS. Rather[13] your eyes must with his judgment
    look.
HERMIA. I do entreat[14] your grace to pardon me.
[...]

Annotations

[1] **our nuptial hour | Draws on apace** – our wedding day will be soon
[2] **wanes** – wears itself out
[3] **steep themselves in** – dissolve into
[4] **solemnities** – wedding ceremonies

[5] **I woo'd thee ... doing thee injuries** – I captured you in war
[6] **With pomp, with triumph and with revelling** – with expensive public celebration
[7] **vexation** – anger

[8] **bewitch'd the bosom of my child** – charmed her heart away
[9] **composed your beauties** – made you as you are
[10] **but as a form in wax | By him imprinted** – he has made nothing but a wax figure

[11] **wanting your father's voice** – without your father's support
[12] **I would** – I wish
[13] **rather** – instead
[14] **I do entreat** – I beg

55 But I beseech your grace that I may know
The worst that may befall me in this case,
If I refuse to wed Demetrius.
THESEUS. Either to die the death or to abjure
For ever the society of men[15].
60 Therefore, fair Hermia, question your desires;
Know of your youth[16], examine well your blood[17],
Whether, if you yield not to[18] your father's choice,
You can endure the livery[19] of a nun,
[...]
65 **HERMIA.** So will I grow, so live, so die, my lord,
Ere I will my virgin patent up[20]
Unto his lordship, whose unwished yoke
My soul consents not to give sovereignty[21].
THESEUS. Take time to pause; and, by the next new
70   moon –
The sealing-day[22] betwixt[23] my love and me,
For everlasting bond of fellowship –
Upon that day either prepare to die
For disobedience to your father's will,
75 Or else to wed Demetrius, as he would[24];
[...]
DEMETRIUS. Relent[25], sweet Hermia: and, Lysander,
   yield
Thy crazed title to my certain right.
80 **LYSANDER.** You have her father's love, Demetrius;
Let me have Hermia's: do you marry him.
EGEUS. Scornful Lysander! true, he hath my love,
And what is mine my love shall render[26] him.
And she is mine, and all my right of her
85 I do estate unto[27] Demetrius.
LYSANDER. I am, my lord, as well derived[28] as he,
As well possess'd[29]; my love is more than his;
My fortunes every way as fairly rank'd,
If not with vantage[30], as Demetrius';
90 And, which is more than all these boasts can be,
I am beloved of beauteous Hermia:

Why should not I then prosecute my right?
Demetrius, I'll avouch it to his head[31],
Made love to[32] Nedar's daughter, Helena,
95 And won her soul; and she, sweet lady, dotes[33],
[...]
Exeunt all but **LYSANDER** *and* **HERMIA**
LYSANDER. How now, my love! why is your cheek
   so pale?
100 How chance the roses there do fade so fast?
HERMIA. Belike[34] for want of rain, which I could well
Beteem[35] them from the tempest of my eyes.
LYSANDER. Ay me! for aught[36] that I could ever read,
Could ever hear by tale or history,
105 The course of true love never did run smooth;
But, either it was different in blood[37], –
HERMIA. O cross![38] too high to be enthrall'd to low[39].
[...]
LYSANDER. Or else it stood upon the choice of
110   friends[40], –
HERMIA. O hell! to choose love by another's eyes.
LYSANDER. Or, if there were a sympathy in choice[41],
War, death, or sickness did lay siege to it,
[...]
115 So quick bright things come to confusion.
HERMIA. If then true lovers have been ever cross'd,
It stands as an edict in destiny:
Then let us teach our trial patience[42],
Because it is a customary cross[43],
120 [...]
LYSANDER. A good persuasion: therefore, hear me,
   Hermia.
I have a widow aunt, a dowager
Of great revenue[44], and she hath no child:
125 From Athens is her house remote seven leagues[45];
And she respects me as her only son.
There, gentle Hermia, may I marry thee;
And to that place the sharp Athenian law
Cannot pursue us. If thou lovest me then,
130 Steal forth thy father's house to-morrow night;

Annotations

[15] **to abjure | For ever the society of men** – to become a nun
[16] **Know of your youth** – think how young you are
[17] **your blood** – your passions
[18] **yield not to** – do not accept
[19] **livery** – uniform, gown
[20] **Ere I will my virgin patent up** – before I give up my virginity
[21] **whose unwished yoke | My soul consents not to give sovereignty** – who I don't want to marry, and have to obey

[22] **sealing-day** – wedding day
[23] **betwixt** – between
[24] **as he would** – as your father wants
[25] **relent** – give up
[26] **render** – give to
[27] **estate unto** – legally transfer to
[28] **as well derived** – from a good family
[29] **as well possess'd** – as rich
[30] **vantage** – advantage, benefit

[31] **avouch it to his head** – say it to his face
[32] **made love to** – courted
[33] **dotes** – loves madly
[34] **belike** – probably, perhaps
[35] **beteem** – bring forth
[36] **for aught** – from anything
[37] **it was different in blood** – the lovers were from different social classes
[38] **O cross!** – What a burden!
[39] **too high to be enthrall'd to low** – too important to be married to a member of a lower social class

[40] **friends** – *here:* relatives, extended family
[41] **if there were a sympathy in choice** – if the lovers could choose each other
[42] **let us teach our trial patience** – put up with it
[43] **it is a customary cross** – it is the normal fate of lovers
[44] **a dowager | Of great revenue** – a rich widow
[45] **remote seven leagues** – 21 miles away

And in the wood, a league without the town,

Where I did meet thee once with Helena,

To do observance to a morn of May,

There will I stay[46] for thee.

135 **HERMIA.** My good Lysander!

I swear to thee, by Cupid's strongest bow,

By his best arrow with the golden head,

By the simplicity[47] of Venus' doves,

By that which knitteth[48] souls and prospers loves,

140 [...]

To-morrow truly will I meet with thee.

LYSANDER. Keep promise, love. Look, here comes

   Helena.

Enter **HELENA**

145 **HERMIA.** God speed[49] fair Helena! Whither away?[50]

HELENA. Call you me fair[51]? that fair again unsay.

Demetrius loves your fair: O happy fair!

Your eyes are lode-stars[52]; and your tongue's sweet air[53]

More tuneable than lark[54] to shepherd's ear,

150 [...]

Sickness is catching: O, were favour so,

Yours would I catch, fair Hermia, ere I go;

My ear should catch your voice, my eye your eye,

My tongue should catch your tongue's sweet melody.

155 Were the world mine, Demetrius being bated[55],

The rest I'd give to be to you translated[56].

O, teach me how you look, and with what art

You sway the motion of Demetrius' heart.

HERMIA. I frown upon him, yet he loves me still.

160 **HELENA.** O that your frowns would teach my smiles

   such skill!

HERMIA. I give him curses, yet he gives me love.

HELENA. O that my prayers could such affection

   move[57]!

165 **HERMIA.** The more I hate, the more he follows me.

HELENA. The more I love, the more he hateth me.

HERMIA. His folly, Helena, is no fault of mine.

HELENA. None, but your beauty: would[58] that fault

   were mine!

170 **HERMIA.** Take comfort: he no more shall see my face;

Lysander and myself will fly this place.

Before the time I did Lysander see,

Seem'd Athens as a paradise to me:

[...]

175 **LYSANDER.** Helen, to you our minds we will unfold[59]:

To-morrow night, when Phoebe[60] doth behold

Her silver visage in the watery glass[61],

Decking[62] with liquid pearl the bladed grass,

A time that lovers' flights doth still conceal,

180 Through Athens' gates have we devised to steal[63].

HERMIA. And in the wood, where often you and I

Upon faint primrose-beds were wont[64] to lie,

Emptying our bosoms[65] of their counsel[66] sweet,

There my Lysander and myself shall meet;

185 And thence[67] from Athens turn away our eyes,

To seek new friends and stranger companies[68].

Farewell, sweet playfellow: pray thou for us;

[...]

LYSANDER. I will, my Hermia.

190 *Exit* **HERMIA**

Helena, adieu:

As you on him, Demetrius dote on[69] you!

Exit

HELENA. How happy some o'er other some[70] can be!

195 Through Athens I am thought as fair as she.

But what of that? Demetrius thinks not so;

He will not know[71] what all but he do know:

And as he errs, doting on Hermia's eyes,

[...]

200 For ere[72] Demetrius look'd on Hermia's eyne[73],

He hail'd down oaths that he was only mine;

And when this hail some heat from Hermia felt,

So he dissolved[74], and showers of oaths did melt.

I will go tell him of fair Hermia's flight:

205 Then to the wood will he to-morrow night

[...]

But herein mean I to enrich[75] my pain,

To have his sight thither[76] and back again. *Exit*

Annotations

[46] **stay** – wait

[47] **simplicity** – sincerity

[48] **knitteth** – joins

[49] **God speed** – bless you

[50] **whither away?** – where are you going?

[51] **fair** – beautiful

[52] **lode-stars** – guiding stars

[53] **air** – voice

[54] **lark** – a songbird

[55] **being bated** – excepted

[56] **to you translated** – transformed into you

[57] **move** – arouse

[58] **would** – I wish

[59] **unfold** – reveal

[60] **Phoebe** – moon goddess

[61] **watery glass** – watery mirror

[62] **decking** – covering

[63] **devised to steal** – planned to slip away

[64] **were wont** – used

[65] **bosoms** – hearts

[66] **counsel** – secrets

[67] **thence** – from then on

[68] **stranger companies** – the company of strangers

[69] **dote on** – idolize, worship

[70] **some o'er other some** – more than others

[71] **will not know** – ignores

[72] **for ere** – before

[73] **eyne** – eyes

[74] **dissolved** – weakened

[75] **enrich** – reward

[76] **thither** – going there

ANALYSIS

4 📖 **SB p. 287/3**

a) Read the information about the common features of a Shakespearean comedy. Then analyse how these characteristics apply to *A Midsummer Night's Dream*.

_____

_____

_____

_____

_____

_____

_____

_____

_____

_____

b) Discuss the major differences between a Shakespearean comedy and a tragedy (e.g. *Romeo and Juliet*).

Info

Common features of a Shakespearean comedy

What makes a Shakespeare comedy identifiable if the genre is not distinct from Shakespearean tragedies and histories? This is an ongoing area of debate, but many believe that the comedies share certain characteristics, as described below:

- **Comedy through language:** Shakespeare's comedies are peppered with clever wordplay, metaphors, and insults.
- **Love:** The theme of love is prevalent in every Shakespeare comedy. Often, we are presented with sets of lovers who, through the course of the play, overcome the obstacles in their relationship and unite. Of course, that measure isn't always foolproof; love is the central theme of *Romeo and Juliet* but few people would regard that play as a comedy.
- **Complex plots:** The plots of Shakespeare comedies have more twists and turns than his tragedies and histories. Although the plots are convoluted, they do follow similar patterns. For example, the climax of the play always occurs in the third act and the final scene has a celebratory feel when the lovers finally declare their feelings for each other.
- **Mistaken identities:** The plot of a Shakespearean comedy is often driven by mistaken identity. Sometimes this is an intentional part of a villain's plot, as in *Much Ado About Nothing* when Don John tricks Claudio into believing that his fiancé has been unfaithful through mistaken identity. Characters also play scenes in disguise and it is not uncommon for female characters to disguise themselves as male characters.

5 **EXTRA**

Act out the scene.

Analysing characters

6   📖 **SB p. 285/7**

a) Read the extract from *Romeo and Juliet* on p. 282-284 in your textbook again and summarize the plot.

b) **Pair work** Partner A notes down the lines of the passages that contain information about Juliet's character. Partner B notes down the lines of the passages that contain information about Romeo's character.

c) Fill in the grid taking into account the passages containing information about your character.

> **Info**
>
> Remember that characters in fictional texts may be developed in two ways:
> - **direct characterization:** The author explicitly states the character's personality traits using descriptive adjectives, adverbs or phrases.
> - **indirect characterization:** The readers have to draw their own conclusions about a character through his or her outward appearance, speech, dialogue, thoughts, actions, interactions with and reactions from other characters.

aspect	information about the character's personality	line(s)
outward appearance		
feelings / attitudes		
speech / dialogue		
relationship to others / interaction		

d) Find suitable adjectives describing your character.

_____

_____

e) Write your characterization, structuring it into introduction, body and conclusion. Remember to support your statements by quoting from the text and giving line references.

f) **Pair work** Present your characterization to your partner.

g) **Pair work** Analyse the similarities and differences between the two characters.

h) **Pair work** Imagine how an actor and an actress would perform the scene. Create a freeze frame.

Henry V: A modern adaption as a graphic novel

1 📖 **SB p. 292/1**

Some of Shakespeare's plays, for example *Henry V*, have been adapted to modern readers in the form of graphic novels.

a) Use the internet to find out about the difference between graphic novels and comics.

b) Look at a page of the graphic novel *Henry V* online. **Webcode** DSW-73067-16

c) Now create a panel (picture) for a graphic novel of King Henry V delivering his speech on his motivational strategies (see p. 292 in your textbook).

d) Comment on the following statement:

> "The future of the graphic novel lies in the choice of worthwhile themes and the innovation of exposition."

Grammar

Definite article and zero article

2 **EXTRA**

Read the following sentences and decide whether you need the definite article or no article at all.

1. Shakespeare is often called _____ English national poet and considered by many to be _____ greatest dramatist of all _____ time.

2. Many of his plays were published in _____ editions of varying quality during his lifetime.

3. Shakespeare most likely attended grammar school. Its curriculum consisted of an intense emphasis on _____ Latin classics, including memorization, writing, and acting out _____ classic Latin plays.

4. _____ classical writers studied in the classroom influenced Shakespeare's work; for example, some of his ideas for _____ plots and characters came from Ovid's tales.

5. _____ Plague broke out in London in _____ 1593, forcing _____ theatres to close.

6. _____ Elizabethan world was in a state of flux and _____ people were confused, frightened and excited about _____ traditional beliefs challenged by scientific discovery and exploration.

7. In Shakespeare's day it was popularly believed that _____ fortunes of everyone and everything were affected by _____ events in _____ heavens.

8. According to _____ Great Chain of Being, God was _____ head of all things; the king, his representative on Earth, was the head of _____ State, and the Pope the head of _____ Church.

Argumentative writing:
Should we stop reading Shakespeare in school?

3 EXTRA

a) Read the following article and outline its main content.

b) State your opinion on the following quotation from the article:

> "The way the plays are taught in many schools is wrong – and most of us should stop trying to read them." (ll. 10-12)

Prepare a line of argument and a thesis statement first. Then, write a discussion consisting of an introduction, a main part and a conclusion (see textbook pp. 338-339 for help).

COLE MORETON   Mail Online, 16 April 2016

'The plays weren't written to be read, they were written to be spoken out loud and acted': Sir Ian McKellen on why it's a waste of time reading Shakespeare and what REALLY irritates him about theatre audiences

What's got into Sir Ian McKellen, the peerless[1] actor who thrilled theatre audiences as King Lear and moviegoers as Richard III? Is he really kicking off our Shakespeare special by calling for a reading ban on
5 *the Bard[2]? [...]*

Nobody knows William Shakespeare better than Sir Ian McKellen. The veteran actor[3] has played all the leading roles, from Romeo and Hamlet to Macbeth and King Lear – so it is a shock to hear
10 him declare that the way the plays are taught in many schools is wrong – and most of us should stop trying to read them.

'Reading Shakespeare is almost as difficult as reading Mozart on the page [from the musical
15 notes],' says McKellen in that deep, warm voice familiar to millions around the world who may never have seen a play by the Bard in their lives. McKellen is a genuine Hollywood superstar: Magneto in the *X-Men* movies and Gandalf in *The*
20 *Hobbit* and *Lord Of The Rings* – the long, pointy hat worn by the kindly wizard sits proudly on a hat stand just inside the door of his home by the river in east London, startling visitors. [...]

McKellen's passion is for William Shakespeare,
25 and he is preparing to lead the celebrations that will mark 400 years since the playwright's death in April 1616. 'If you're telling the story of Othello and Iago, then you're telling the story of lives that are still current,' he said. [...]
30 'Much has changed in the past 400 years but human nature hasn't really changed,' he declares. 'We're all susceptible[4] to falling in love and out of love, being

jealous, envious, ambitious. So if you're telling the story of Othello and Iago, say, then you're telling
35 the story of lives that are still current.'

Incredibly, though, McKellen wants us all to put down our books and stop trying to learn the plays before we've seen them.

'It's not what ordinary people should have to bother
40 with. That's for the actors to do. The plays weren't written to be read, they were written to be spoken out loud and acted and for us as an audience to watch.'

Seeing a play first makes the words come alive,
45 he insists. 'If you see Shakespeare on stage, much of the difficulty goes. You may not understand every word but you get more than the gist, and long stretches of the plays are perfectly easy to understand.'
50 Too many of us are put off Shakespeare at school by having to stare at pages of blank verse wondering what it's all about, he says. 'It's a great pity if people who are new to Shakespeare, whatever their age, have to read him. They should go and see him.'
55 Sir Ian is no fan of teaching Shakespeare by the book – as is still the case in the majority of schools. 'It worries me that you might easily be put off Shakespeare for life if that's how you start out,' he said. [...] 'I find it very difficult to read a play, even
60 now. If I get a new one I have to hear it out loud before I can judge what it's like.'

[...]

'The idea of any children in their early teens with a teacher who has not quite worked out how to

Annotations
[1] **peerless** (adj) – having no equals
[2] **the Bard** (n) – *here:* William Shakespeare
[3] **veteran actor** (n) – very experienced actor
[4] **susceptible** (adj) – inclined

65 do this, so that it just comes down to reading and reading, perhaps speaking it out loud, maybe even standing up and acting out a little bit … it worries me that you might easily be put off Shakespeare for life if that's how you start out.' […]

70 Not all of us can afford to go to the theatre, which is why he has worked with collaborators to come up with an astonishing new app for the iPad that brings the theatre to your lap.

It's all very modern for a 76-year-old who is often
75 described as our Greatest Living Shakespearean, though he laughs when I mention that people say such things. […]

The big question people have been asking for years – and which is resurfacing⁵ as the anniversary
80 approaches – is this: who exactly was Shakespeare, really? […]

'It's clear that Shakespeare wrote plays with other people, that's in the nature of the job. Odd as it may sound, every episode of [the American sitcom] *Will*
85 *& Grace* is written by 12 people. There are 20 people who write *Coronation Street*. I did ten episodes and each was written by a different author, but the audience couldn't tell, they were brilliant at it.'

His friends believe Shakespeare was too poorly
90 educated to have written the plays himself.

'Does it matter? It's evident to me that the man who wrote the plays loved the theatre. He thinks as an actor. One of Shakespeare's greatest contributions to human thought is that "All the world's a stage
95 and all the men and women merely players". Human beings act. Animals don't act. We disguise ourselves, we pretend. That all seems to add up to being some professional who was well steeped in theatre and doing this as a full-time job.' […]

100 'My parents went to the theatre a lot – it was my main hobby as a child. I was never frightened of Shakespeare, bewildered or overwhelmed by him.'

His first encounter was at the Little Theatre in his home town of Wigan when his big sister took him
105 to see *Twelfth Night*⁶ at the age of nine. 'As she told me a bit of the story in advance, I didn't have any difficulty.'

But it was at Cambridge that he first came across the challenge of a heckler⁷ in the audience and he
110 was shocked.

'The first time I walked on the stage as an undergraduate at the amateur dramatic club, some drunk who had just wandered into the theatre shouted, "Get off!" That was the first comment I
115 ever heard from an audience.'

Annotations
⁵ to **resurface** (v) – to appear again
⁶ *Twelfth Night* – romantic comedy by William Shakespeare
⁷ **heckler** (n) – someone who interrupts a public performance with loud, unfriendly statements
⁸ **accessible** (adj) – *here:* understandable, comprehensible

There were more annoying disturbances when he began to play the leading roles such as Romeo and Hamlet. 'It can be very distracting if you're playing Hamlet and there's somebody on the front
120 row with the script, not looking at you. Listening to you, following the text, turning the page and saying, "You've missed something out." All actors will say you can start a famous speech and there will be someone in the audience saying the words
125 at the same time.' […]

McKellen prefers performing in small theatres because they are intimate. He believes in diversity but admits that theatre audiences are still predominantly white.

130 Isn't there a real danger that Shakespeare remains the preserve of rich, middle-class people who can afford up to £100 a time to see it?

'Yes, and I think that's addressed by making sure there are some, if not many, cheap tickets. It's not
135 ideal, I suppose. But it's not got to the stage that opera has got to.'

He points to videos of past productions and cinema screenings of live productions as examples of ways in which Shakespeare has been made more
140 accessible⁸.

And of course there are proper movies, although you've got to be careful with those, says McKellen. 'A film can be useful but the text can be cut to the bone.'

145 All this has been weighing heavily on his mind, but McKellen has come up with his own remarkable – and potentially game-changing – solution to the problem of how to get more people to love Shakespeare.

150 He has developed a new app for the iPad with Heuristic Media that takes the user into the rehearsal room for an intimate performance of the play.

Actors speak their parts directly to the camera,
155 while the words scroll down at the same pace on the bottom half of the screen. […]

'Everybody who uses the app says, "Oh, I see. Yes, this makes it easier." This is the equivalent of getting a Mozart manuscript then seeing and
160 hearing the orchestra play.' […]

'It wouldn't make the plays any better for us to realise one day that Shakespeare was a woman,' says McKellen, finishing with the flourish of a quote from Hamlet. 'It would be interesting but the
165 plays would remain. The play's the thing!'

Exam 1 – Britishness
Part A: Viewing/Listening

Webcode DSW-73067-17

Listen to a news report from 2013 about the question of how people in the Northern English areas Redcar & Cleveland and Middlesbrough feel about the issue of immigration. Then complete the listening tasks.

1 *Listen to the sequence from 00:00 to 02:29 again. While listening, tick (✓) the correct answers. There can be more than one correct answer.*

a) What is true about Redcar and Cleveland?
- ❑ It is an area with many immigrants.
- ❑ There used to be a lot of industry.
- ❑ It used to be a tourist area.
- ❑ Many people have jobs in the tourist industry.

b) What is the first couple's opinion on immigrants?
- ❑ Immigrants are not a problem at all.
- ❑ In the area (Redcar and Cleveland) there are not many immigrants.
- ❑ The people in the area are afraid of immigrants being thieves.
- ❑ Romanians come with best intentions.

c) Next Fatima Manji interviews two elderly ladies. They say:
- ❑ Many people feel upset because they themselves do not have a job.
- ❑ Many believe immigrants who get there will be unemployed.
- ❑ There will be more immigrants than British people.
- ❑ Middlesbrough is a good example for integration.

2 *Listen to the sequence from 02:30 to 03:06 again. While listening, complete the sentences.*

a) One of the few immigrants to the area is called Reginald Peter. He says he now feels _____.

b) But he has _____.

c) Some say the harsh political climate is hardening people's views towards migrants.

_____ remains high in the area, especially among _____.

3 *Listen to the sequence from 03:07 to 04:15 again. While listening, tick (✓) true or false. If false, correct the statement.*

	true	false
a) A young lady believes a lot of racists blame foreigners for being without a job.	❑	❑
b) The expected arrival of Bulgarians and Romanians is a concern because some think houses are already being prepared for the new migrants.	❑	❑
c) The local councillor says this is right and they have empty houses waiting for migrants.	❑	❑

4 *Listen to the sequence from* **04:16** *to* **05:17** *again. While listening, complete the sentences.*

a) Romanians living in Middlesbrough are _____ about the way they are being

_____ .

b) When talking to them, Fatima Manji learns that it is _____ that many Romanians

have been preparing to come to England starting with January 1st.

c) Fatima Manji says that many Romanians feel _____ and _____ .

d) Fatima Manji in the end finds it striking that a place _____ could

produce such strong feelings against immigration.

Webcode DSW-73067-18

The podcast series "Talking Migration" deals with discussions, debates and interviews on the politics of
migration. In episode number 5 "Brexit or Bremain?", Dr. Andy Mycock from the University of Huddersfield
discusses topics like Britishness and reasons why the British could vote for "remain" or "leave" shortly before
the Brexit referendum of 2016. Listen to the sequence from **01:00** to **04:10**. Then complete the listening task.

5 *Listen again. While listening, complete the sentences.*

a) Andy Mycock says the referendum debate is framed around the _____ implications

of leaving or remaining part of the European Union and also about the role of _____ .

b) He points out that the UK has recently gone through the experience of the Scottish _____

referendum, which shows that the UK itself is fragile and could easily _____ .

c) Mycock thinks the tone of the debate has changed with the serial _____, which

have raised questions about the extent to which the UK is a secular _____ having a

fundamental Christian religious institutional framework.

d) Andy Mycock talks about the question whether immigration is reinforcing a sense of _____

_____ or whether it is rather undermining it.

e) Many British feel that Britain is _____ in some ways. Britishness is either framed by

a sense of _____ or is framed against it.

f) Mycock thinks that actually the referendum debate is as much a debate about what it means to be British

in the _____ as it is about what it means _____ .

Part B: Reading/Writing

Read the following article carefully, then do the tasks below.

RACHEL CONOLLY   The Guardian, 26 May 2020

Reversing the brain drain[1]: why coronavirus could stop graduates[2] moving to London

My grandma, who lives in Derry[3], had never been to England until last year, so it was a great honour when she made the trip to London to visit me and my sister, who have both lived on the mainland (in one city or another) for the best part of a decade. We had "great craic[4]" during her stay. [...]

That was almost a year ago and I haven't seen her in person since. I'm always a bit jealous of people for whom family get-togethers like these aren't a rarity. As they are for many young people in the UK who grew up outside of the economic hub[5] of the south-east, the job prospects in the region where I'm from are, shall we say, not great. So, like many young people, I moved away for university, then to London for work, and now my life feels awkwardly spread across several versions of home. I don't see most of my family as much as I'd like [...].

The well-trodden path of young people moving to London was detailed in a 2016 report, the Great British Brain Drain, which found that almost a quarter of all UK graduates from the three previous years were working in London within six months of graduating. [...]

The report discussed this "brain drain" mostly in terms of the negative economic impact it has on the regions that young people leave, but there is a social and cultural one too, which is harder to quantify. I've often thought about this and discussed it with friends in similar positions, but the first time I saw any reference to it written down was in *New Model Island*, a book by Alex Niven. In it, he described the "profound emotional and practical difficulties that come with being uprooted[6] from successive locales" experienced by young people from places such as "Liverpool, Newport or Belfast" who move constantly in search of work. [...]

Young people from London who aren't born wealthy fare no better (as Niven also points out), as they are forced out of the boroughs they grew up in (if not the city itself) by ever-rising rents. [...] Professional life in the UK orbits[7] around the south east; and while politicians may speak of the need to regenerate "left behind" areas in the rest of the country around election time, it seems unlikely that this government will affect meaningful change any time soon. But now the pandemic has prompted[8] this mass experiment in home working, it seems a shift in the relationship between UK geography and job opportunities doesn't have to be led by the government.

Since the UK started taking the coronavirus seriously, in late March [of 2020], we've seen many societal changes [...]. Almost overnight, most people who work in an office were sent home, and it now seems clear that many could do their job remotely[9], if not all the time, then at least for most it. Several big tech companies [...], including Facebook and Twitter, have already said employees will be given the option to work remotely for good[10]. A set-up in which people work from home or a local co-working space and commute to the main office once or twice a month seems feasible[11] for a lot of "knowledge" work, and if this does end up filtering out to other industries it would not be the worst thing for the UK's regional divide and the rising cost of living in London. [...] This could be a chance to reset.

Annotations

1. **brain drain** (n) – *here:* the sucking of talent and highly qualified young people from the rest of the country, which causes a drain in those areas
2. **graduate** (n) – someone who has finished university
3. **Derry** – second biggest city in Northern Ireland
4. **great craic** – Irish expression for "a good time"
5. **hub** (n) – *here:* centre
6. to **uproot** (v) – *German:* entwurzeln
7. to **orbit** (v) – *German:* umkreisen
8. to **prompt** sth (v) – *German:* der Anlass zu etwas sein
9. **remotely** (adv) – from somewhere else than from the office, e.g. from home office
10. **for good** (adv) – forever, definitely
11. **feasible** (adj) – practicable, possible

6   Summarize the article. (*comprehension*)

7   Analyse the author's train of thought, her use of language and its effect. (*analysis*)

8   Write a letter to the editor commenting on Conolly's opinion that coronavirus and working remotely could stop London from draining brain and being the centre of Britain. (*re-creation of text*)

Part C: Mediation

9 A British friend of yours has just written you an email telling you that he / she heard about Angela Merkel's farewell visit to the Queen in July 2021. He / she wants to know what the Germans think about the Queen. Now write back, outlining the information from the article below.

Abendzeitung München, 19. Juni 2015

Warum die Deutschen so verrückt nach ihr sind

Königinnen mag es so einige geben. Aber es gibt nur eine Queen. [...] Woher kommt diese Begeisterung für eine im Grunde genommen eher unauffällige ältere Dame?

Sie ist [...] Handtaschenträgerin und mehrfache Uroma. Sie sagt nicht allzu viel und verfügt, soweit bekannt, über keine herausragenden Fähigkeiten.

Aber sie ist eben englische Queen, und allein aufgrund
5 dieser Tatsache versetzt sie ganze Völkerscharen in Entzücken. Ganz besonders die Deutschen. Denn Elizabeth Windsor und ihre lieben Verwandten sprechen gleich mehrere deutsche Sehnsüchte an:

DIE SEHNSUCHT NACH DER MONARCHIE:

10 „Die Krone fiel – wer wird denn weinen?", fragte Kurt Tucholsky, als die Deutschen ihren eigenen Royal Kaiser Wilhelm 1918 ins Exil schickten. Aber es fehlte dann doch was. Für Hans-Dieter Gelfert, Autor zahlreicher England-Bücher, ist es offensichtlich, „dass die Deutschen ihre
15 latente Sehnsucht nach der Monarchie auf die britische Krone projizieren". In einer Wettbewerbsgesellschaft zählen Monarchen zu den wenigen Menschen, die man bewundern kann, ohne sich unterlegen zu fühlen, denn, so Gelfert zur Deutschen Presse-Agentur: „Als König
20 bzw. Königin wird man geboren – oder auch nicht."

DIE SEHNSUCHT NACH KULTURELLER EINHEIT:

Die Queen bildet den kulturellen Mittelpunkt Englands. Die Engländer empfinden auf diese Weise eine Verbundenheit mit ihren Landsleuten, die sich zum
25 Beispiel in zahllosen privat organisierten Straßenfesten zu den Thronjubiläen manifestiert. Die Deutschen erleben ein solches Gemeinschaftsgefühl wohl nur bei Erfolgen der Fußball-Nationalmannschaft.

DIE SEHNSUCHT NACH DER KLASSEN-
30 GESELLSCHAFT:

Die Fernsehserie „Downton Abbey", ein weltweiter Exportschlager, zeigt das spätfeudale Herrschaftsbiotop einer englischen Adelsfamilie. Der Erfolg der Serie lässt sich wohl nur erklären mit einer geheimen Sehnsucht
35 vieler Menschen nach der damaligen Gesellschaft, in der jeder seinen Platz kannte. Das Symbol dieses Modells ist die Königin von England, die zu berühren bis heute tabu ist.

DIE SEHNSUCHT NACH STIL:

40 Viele Deutsche bewundern die englische Aristokratie für ihren Stil. Diese ganzen manierierten Sprach- und Verhaltenscodes, dieses unnachahmliche Original-Geschnösel der Upperclass, aber auch der trockene Humor. Man denke nur daran, was die englische Queen
45 einmal zu einer bürgerlichen Gesprächspartnerin sagte, deren Handy während ihrer Unterhaltung unaufhörlich klingelte: „Sie sollten rangehen. Vielleicht ist es jemand Wichtiges."

DIE SEHNSUCHT NACH DEM ZEREMONIELL:

50 Die Deutschen lieben das britische Königshaus nicht zuletzt für „Pomp and Circumstance" – und übertragen deshalb jede sich bietende Hochzeit oder Beerdigung live auf mehreren Kanälen. „Es gibt eine Sehnsucht nach dem Zeremoniell", sagt der britische Botschafter Simon
55 McDonald im dpa-Interview.

DIE SEHNSUCHT NACH MORALISCHER INTEGRITÄT:

Die britische Monarchie ist ein Big-Brother-Haus, aus dem man nie wieder rauskommt. Die Mitglieder dieser
60 Familie stehen unter ständiger Medienbeobachtung, und das ist der zwischenmenschlichen Beziehung nicht unbedingt förderlich. Bekanntermaßen ist im Laufe der Jahre so einiges in die Brüche gegangen. Die hormonell gesteuerten Wirrungen des Windsor-Clans haben der
65 Rest-Welt schon viele heitere Stunden im ärztlichen Wartezimmer beschert – wobei sich die englische Queen nie etwas zuschulden kommen ließ. Sie ist immer ein moralisches Vorbild geblieben.

DIE SEHNSUCHT NACH KONTINUITÄT:

70 1953 war das Jahr, in dem Josef Stalin starb, ein VW Käfer 4200 Mark kostete und der 1. FC Kaiserslautern Deutscher Fußballmeister wurde. So ziemlich alles hat sich seit damals geändert – nur nicht die Frau auf dem britischen Thron.

Exam 2 – Postcolonial experiences
Part A: Listening

Webcode DSW-73067-19
Listen to a radio interview with the Jamaican author Marlon James from Kingston. Then complete the listening tasks.

1 *While listening, fill in the missing information. You do not need to write complete sentences.*

a) **Suburban Kingston**
   Name eight major negative facts about the city in the 1970s.

   _____   _____

   _____   _____

   _____   _____

   _____   _____

b) **Signs of hope**
   Name four positive developments in "Kingston Town" during the same period.

   _____

   _____

   _____

   _____

c) **Criticizing the local police force**
   According to the interviewee, what were the major characteristics of the Jamaican police force back then?

   _____

   _____

d) **Post-post-colonialism**
   According to Marlon James, what are the major characteristics of post-post-colonialism?

   _____

   _____

   _____

   _____

Part B: Reading/Writing

Read the following article carefully, then do the tasks on p. 119.

SOUTIK BISWAS   BBC India, 8 July 2021

Pew survey: India is neither a melting pot nor a salad bowl

For long, societies have been described as melting pots and salad bowls.

Annotations
1 to **fuse** (v) – to melt, to blend
2 to **retain** (v) – to keep
3 **lead** (adj) – *here:* main
4 to **flounder** (v) – to struggle badly
5 **fault line** (n) – *German:* Bruchlinie
6 to **dwindle** (v) – to become less

The first encourage immigrants to fuse[1] into a dominant culture; in the second, immigrants retain[2] their own characteristics while integrating into a new society. India is apparently neither, according to a new study by US-based Pew Research Center. The non-profit fact tank has released this comprehensive survey on religion in India after talking to some 30,000 people in 17 languages. Hindus make up 80% of the population, while Muslims comprise 14%.

When it comes to religion, the study finds that Indians of all faiths support, at once, religious tolerance *and* religious segregation. The majority (84%) say that "respect" for other religions is an important part of their identity and to being truly Indian. Yet a substantial number of them do not want neighbours who belong to another religion [...]. They also prefer making friends within their own religious community. "This points to a unique understanding of plurality of Indian society – it is more like a *thali* (an Indian meal comprising a selection of separate dishes served on a platter), rather than a melting pot," says Neha Sahgal, one of the lead[3] authors of the study.

Many scholars believe India's founding fathers wanted a society which was more a salad bowl, where the national identity recognised and accommodated a diverse group of citizens. So has this dream floundered[4] and has India turned out to be a complex republic, a patchwork quilt of people, religions and cultures where people live together, but separately? It is difficult to say. Despite the strongly held desire for religious segregation, Indians share a lot of beliefs. For instance, most Hindus (81%) believe the holy Ganges river has the power to purify. But so do 66% of Jains, a quarter of Muslims and a third of Christians. [...] "It is

not uncommon to see seemingly contradictory viewpoints in public opinion," Jonathan Evans, the second lead author of the study told me. In West Europe, for example, a 2019 Pew study found that Christians – whether they attended church regularly or not – were more likely than people with no religious identity to have negative views of religious minorities and immigrants. The results led many to wonder how this fitted the Christian doctrine of "to love thy neighbour" and actions of West European churches to actively resettle refugees from the Middle East. [...]

In India, scholars said, religious segregation was closely tied to the fault lines[5] of national identity and politics. [...] Is that leading to discrimination against the minorities? According to the survey, about a quarter of followers of any of the major faiths said they had faced a lot of discrimination. [...] More worryingly, a majority (65%) of Indians – Hindus and Muslims almost equally – said religious violence was a "very big problem". Only corruption, crime and violence against women ranked higher as issues of concern. Surprisingly, only 20% believed discrimination on the basis of caste was widespread. "It is quite possible for an exclusionary society to think it is not discriminating [...]," noted Pratap Bhanu Mehta, a leading scholar. So what does this survey – the largest conducted by Pew outside US – tell us about India?

Analysts like Prof Mehta believe it reveals a religious nation which is committed to diversity, but also an exclusionary one with dwindling[6] support for individual freedom and an increasing commitment to Hindu politics.

More broadly, according to Hilal Ahmed, a scholar on political Islam, the survey reinforces the fact that India is a "conservative society in a democratic framework".

2 Outline the main findings of the Pew study as reported in the article. (*comprehension*)

3 Analyse how the author uses language and communicative strategies to make the findings of the Pew study interesting to the reader. (*analysis*)

4 Choose **one** of the following tasks. (*comment/discussion*)

a) Hilal Ahmed, a scholar on political Islam, describes India as a "conservative society in a democratic framework" (ll. 79f.). Explain what he means by that and comment on this statement.

b) Read the following definition of a "melting pot" and a "salad bowl". Discuss the benefits and drawbacks of each concept for society.

> A **salad bowl** [...] is a metaphor for the way a multicultural society can integrate different cultures while maintaining their separate identities, contrasting with a **melting pot**, which emphasizes the combination of the parts into a single whole. *(Wikipedia)*

Part C: Mediation

You are taking part in an international school convention on postcolonial experiences called "Justice now!". As a German student, you prepare an article about Germany's colonial past and its aftermath. Give an outline of what happened on behalf of German colonialist policy in the early 20th century and describe what steps the German government takes today to assume responsibility. Don't forget to explain why this policy has its limits and is criticized as well.

Deutsche Kolonialvergangenheit
Namibia: Deutschland erkennt Völkermord an

Andreas Kynast und Katharina Thode, zdf.de
27.05.2021

Nach 113 Jahren steht Deutschland vor einem historischen Schritt: Bundestag und Bundesregierung erkennen den Völkermord an Herero und Nama an und wollen um Vergebung bitten.

5 Nach sechs Jahren und neun Gesprächsrunden steht fest: Deutschland wird die Verbrechen des deutschen Kaiserreichs an Herero und Nama als Völkermord anerkennen. Die Bundesregierung hat sich dazu verpflichtet, die „politisch-moralische"
10 Verantwortung für die Gräueltaten deutscher Kolonialtruppen zu übernehmen. Die Nachkommen will sie mit einem Milliardenbetrag unterstützen.
Namibia begrüßte diesen Schritt. Die Anerkennung der Verbrechen sei „der erste Schritt in die richtige
15 Richtung", sagte ein Sprecher von Präsident Hage Geingob. Kritik äußerte die Opposition in Namibia. Deutsche Vertreter hätten „nicht in gutem Glauben gehandelt", sagte die Abgeordnete Inna Hengari. Bundesaußenminister Heiko Maas begrüße

20 die „Einigung über den gemeinsamen Umgang mit dem dunkelsten Kapitel unserer gemeinsamen Geschichte". Er erläuterte die Zuwendungen als Geste der Anerkennung des unermesslichen Leids, das den Opfern zugefügt wurde.
25 Die Bundesregierung wolle Namibia und die Nachkommen der Opfer „mit einem substanziellen Programm in Höhe von 1,1 Milliarden Euro zum Wiederaufbau und zur Entwicklung unterstützen", sagte Maas (SPD) am Freitag.
30 Die Bundesregierung hat mit Landes- und Opfervertretern aus Namibia eine Erklärung verfasst, die die Anerkennung festhält. Eine solche Vereinbarung ist historisch ohne Beispiel und sowohl politisch als auch rechtlich Neuland. Die Erklärung ist nun unter-
35 schriftsreif – zudem sind erste Details zu den Inhalten bekannt.

**Die deutsch-namibische Aussöhnungs-
deklaration**

• **Anerkennung des Völkermordes:** In der
40 Erklärung bezeichnet die Bundesregierung

die Verbrechen des deutschen Kaiserreichs an den Herero und Nama als Völkermord. Für Deutschland wichtig: Ein Rechtsanspruch leitet sich daraus nicht ab, um nicht unter die später
45 erlassene UN-Konvention und die daraus folgende Bestrafung zu fallen.

- **Entschädigung:** Deutschland sagt „substantielle" Mittel für ein Wiederaufbau- und Zukunftsprogramm zu, das den Nachfahren
50 der damaligen Opfer zugutekommen soll. Die Höhe der Zahlungen beläuft sich auf 1,1 Milliarden Euro in den nächsten 30 Jahren. Die Mittel sollen zum Beispiel für den Landkauf, die Landentwicklung, die Wasserversorgung und
55 Berufsausbildung eingesetzt werden.
- **Erinnerung und Aufbau:** Außerdem soll eine gemeinsame Stiftung zur Erinnerung und Zukunftsgestaltung gegründet werden.

Teile der Herero kritisieren die Verhandlungen

60 Die Reaktionen auf die Erklärung dürften in Namibia allerdings gemischt ausfallen. Das liegt vor allem an der Zusammensetzung der Gesprächspartner: Teile der Herero kritisieren seit Beginn der Gespräche im Jahr 2015, dass sie selbst nicht mit am Verhand-
65 lungstisch sitzen durften. Ein Teil der Herero hatte die Bundesrepublik deshalb vor einem Gericht in New York verklagt.
Deutschland habe auf die Zusammensetzung der namibischen Delegation nur sehr begrenzten Ein-
70 fluss, heißt es aus Diplomatenkreisen zu diesem Vorwurf. Bei Regierungsverhandlungen sei es üblich, dass die Vertreter von der jeweiligen Seite bestimmt würden.

Der Völkermord an den Herero und Nama

75 Aus existenzieller Not heraus erhoben sich im einstigen Deutsch-Südwestafrika von 1904 bis 1908 die Herero gegen die deutsche Kolonialmacht. Unter Generalleutnant Lothar von Trotha schlug eine rund 15.000 Soldaten umfassende Streitmacht
80 die Rebellion der Einheimischen innerhalb weniger Monate militärisch nieder. So ließ der deutsche Befehlshaber in der „Schlacht am Waterberg" einen

Großteil der Herero einkesseln und vernichten. Zudem ließ er die wasserlose Omaheke-Wüste abrie-
85 geln, in die Tausende Herero geflohen waren. Die Flüchtlinge verdursteten.
Später gab von Trotha den Vernichtungsbefehl: „Innerhalb der deutschen Grenzen wird jeder Herero mit oder ohne Gewehr erschossen. Ich nehme
90 keine Weiber und Kinder mehr auf, treibe sie zu ihrem Volk zurück oder lasse auf sie schießen." Etwa 65.000 der 80.000 Herero und mindestens 10.000 der 20.000 Nama wurden damals getötet.

Wie geht es jetzt weiter?

95 Die Erklärung soll in Kürze von beiden Außenministern in Windhoek unterzeichnet werden. Sie soll noch vor der Bundestagswahl an die Parlamente gehen. In der zweiten Jahreshälfte will Bundespräsident Frank-Walter Steinmeier im Parlament Nami-
100 bias um Vergebung bitten – Namibia, so heißt es, will der Bitte nachkommen.